THE BRILLIANT ART OF
PEACE

Contents

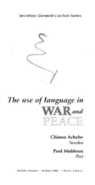

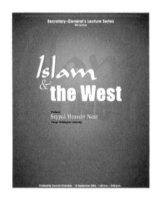

Posters designed by the Graphic Design Unit, Department of Public Information, United Nations.

Foreword

During my tenure as secretary-general of the United Nations, I measured the success of United Nations programs and activities not only in terms of meeting the expectations of member states, but also in how they affected the lives of people. I believed that engaging broader constituencies such as civil society organizations, business, and academic institutions was important to help fulfill the organization's mission. I was also convinced that ideas can change the lives of individuals, reinvigorate institutions, and help achieve a fairer, more secure world for all.

From June 2002 to December 2006, I hosted a series of public lectures on cutting-edge topics in both the humanities and natural sciences for the diplomats of permanent missions to the United Nations, the staff of the UN Secretariat and various funds and programs, and, of course, the nongovernmental organizations accredited to the UN. I thought the lectures would contribute to the ongoing effort within the United Nations to form a common framework of understanding. Such a framework could help ameliorate the cultural and political differences that so often make dialogue and mutual understanding difficult to achieve.

My other goal was to strengthen the sense of community among all of us who work at the United Nations. I knew from long experience as a staff member that one met many people every day in the normal course of work, and knew many others only slightly, or not at all, because of different assignments or specialties. Yet, there were issues, in areas like the natural sciences or the humanities, that we were all interested in outside our regular duties. I wanted the lectures to inform, to stimulate, and to challenge the members of the United Nations family.

The speakers are eminent individuals from a wide range of disciplines and regions. The lectures focused on a broad range of topics: the humanities, language, music, globalization, human rights, identity, religion, science and technology, and the United Nations. Not surprisingly, the speakers helped us answer important questions with their wisdom, experience, and clarity.

I am deeply grateful to all of them for their important contributions. And I am glad that the lectures, which spanned four eventful years in world affairs, have been collected together in this volume for others to enjoy.

Kofi A. Annan

Introduction

ABIODUN WILLIAMS

The secretary-generalship of the United Nations is a position that eight men have held in nearly seventy years. The first secretary-general, Trygve Lie, observed that it is "the most impossible job on this earth." Whether that assessment is true or not, it was the most famous thing he ever said. And there is a case for it. The office has authority but no power in the strict sense of the word. The power of the office lies in its moral authority, and the actual impact on events and the achievement of tangible results depend on how this valuable resource is used.

To a greater degree than any of his predecessors, Kofi Annan, the UN's seventh secretary-general, sought to engage not only with member states, but also with global constituencies. He reached out to Nobel laureates, academics, entertainers, and other opinion shapers. He recognized their enormous potential not only as advocates, but valued partners in achieving the goals of the UN. This openness to new constituencies and ideas generated useful ferment in the bureaucracy, and it meant that distinguished speakers were more willing to be associated with the

UN. In was in that spirit that he established the Secretary-General's Lecture Series in 2002.

Obviously, the substance of the lectures is their most significant quality. But first it is important to consider the forum in which they were delivered. The UN is an indispensable forum in which 193 sovereign states, including the powerful and less powerful, can voice their opinions and develop common strategies for tackling global problems. It is also an instrument for implementing those strategies. As the world organization, the UN has unique legitimacy and one of its cardinal functions is to legitimize decisions, values, and principles governing international order. When Chinua Achebe spoke at the UN, he described the organization as a "great shrine of peace and cooperation among nations."

In his lecture, Stephen Schlesinger underlined the central role the United States played in the founding of the UN at the historic conference in San Francisco in 1945. America's support and leadership have always been crucial to a strong and effective UN. Schlesinger expressed a firm belief that despite all the flaws and limitations that were evident even in San Francisco, the UN remains an essential instrument in our world that must be preserved and improved.

The work of the UN is about peace and security, sustainable development, human rights, the rule of law, good governance, and humanitarian assistance. But it is more than that: it is about humanity. And that means it is also about literature, music, and art. When Toni Morrison delivered the inaugural lecture in the series on June 24, 2002, close to one thousand people were in attendance in the Economic and Social Council Chamber to listen to the internationally acclaimed winner of the Nobel Prize for Literature. Kofi Annan put it this way: "Literature has the power to transform us in ways that politics never can. And few writers have demonstrated that power more magically than Toni Morrison, in her wonderful novels." The wounds from the tragic events of September 11 were still fresh. The implications of the terrorist attacks for the United States, the United Nations, and the world were being vigorously debated. The UN was experiencing what would turn out to be a brief period of global unity before the deep divisions over the Iraq war cast their shadow over the organization. Morrison chose "The Humanities after 9/11" as her theme. Her message was clear: "I am convinced that the language that has the most force, that requires the more acumen, talent, grace, genius, and, yes, beauty, can never be, will never again be, found in paeans to the glory of war or erotic rallying cries to battle. The power of this alternative language does not arise from the tiresome, wasteful art of war, but, rather, from the demanding, brilliant art of peace."

Leon Botstein was the only college president and conductor of a symphony orchestra to deliver a lecture in the series. He recalled that the UN has inspired composers such as Aaron Copland. who used the words of the Charter in his *Preamble for a Solemn Occasion*, written to mark the first anniversary of the Universal Declaration of Human Rights. Music does not have the power to end conflict but it can promote dialogue. In a world of diversity where often values clash, music can unite people of different cultural backgrounds. Botstein declared, "Music may . . . be the last refuge of hope beyond language because it is in every human being."

Many of the lectures addressed some aspect of globalization with its challenges and opportunities. Societies in different parts of the world are interacting more deeply and rapidly than ever before. This offers many opportunities, such as access to new international markets and investments for groups or countries able to seize them. The benefits of globalization are unequally distributed, however, and millions of people are denied the chance to reap its rewards. Large parts of humanity also remain outside the global market, half the world's population living on less than $2 a day. It is in the developing countries of Africa, Asia, and Latin America where the incomes are lowest and inequality the greatest.

The lectures "Globalization: Winners and Losers" by Jagdish Bhagwati, Jeffrey Sachs, and Nobel laureate Joseph Stiglitz were delivered on March 14, 2003, during a time of great anxiety over the possibility of war in Iraq. Five days later, U.S. President George W. Bush ordered an air strike against Saddam Hussein, and the ground war in Iraq began the following day. The lectures were a reminder that the promotion of economic growth, sustainable development, and social justice were as central to the UN's work as preventing, managing, and resolving violent conflict.

The United Nations has championed the rights of individuals in a world where international relations are no longer a matter of states alone but involve peoples as well, as the opening words of the Charter imply. However, for millions of people around the world, human rights remain a dream rather than a reality. The debate on the human rights role of the UN has not always been constructive, and the old Commission on Human Rights, since replaced by the Human Rights Council, was largely discredited. William Schulz's lecture made the sobering argument that almost everyone including governments, military officials, the business community, and even the human rights community is afraid of human rights. Although imperfect, the Human Rights Council has raised human rights to the prominence accorded to them by the UN Charter. With the Security Council, the Economic and Social Council, and the Human Rights Council, the intergovernmental machinery of the UN is aligned with the three main priorities in the work of the organization: security, development, and human rights.

Archbishop Tutu's lecture was important as a compelling account of the relationship between religion and politics, and the need for inter-religious understanding and dialogue. He played a critical role in ending apartheid, and in creating today's multiracial South Africa. In one of the darkest periods of the antiapartheid struggle, his efforts were recognized with the award of the Nobel Peace Prize in 1984. Repeatedly throughout history, religion has been used to stoke the fires of hatred and intolerance and to instigate conflict. But at the core of all the great religions are the values of compassion and decency. Devotion does not mean intolerance. Faith does not mean prejudice.

Kofi Annan invited Amartya Sen, a Nobel laureate and one of his economic advisers, and Kwame Anthony Appiah, one of the most distinguished philosophers of his generation, to deliver lectures on "Identity in the Twenty-First Century" in June 2006. The two intellectuals had recently published books on the subject: Sen's *Identity and Violence: The Illusion of Destiny* and Appiah's *Cosmopolitanism: Ethics in a World of Strangers*. Everyone has multiple or overlapping identities, but, as Sen pointed out, the tendency of people in the contemporary world to think that one of these identities—religion, nationality, language, or race—trumps all the others has led to racial violence, communal strife, denial of basic human rights, and religion-related terrorism. Appiah described the universalistic nature of cosmopolitanism and its respect for a wide range of legitimate human diversity. He stressed the importance of dialogue: "Conversation across identities, across religions, races, ethnicities and nationalities is worthwhile because through conversation you can learn from people with different, even incompatible, ideas from your own."

Eric Wieschaus, a Nobel laureate and a world-renowned pioneer in the field of genetics, provided a valuable perspective at a time when the member states of the UN were deeply divided on the issue of cloning. Annan titled his lecture "Designer Genes: The Ethics of Modern Genetics" to suggest a future in which it might be possible to select human genes and predetermine human traits.

All the lectures in this volume illuminate important issues, bring new interpretations to old questions, broaden horizons, and get us to think. The reader will find erudite language, humor, moral rigor, and wit.

The volume is arranged according to broad themes: literature and music, economics and human rights, identity and religion, science and technology, and the United Nations. Within each section, the arrangement is also broadly thematic, not chronological.

A brief note about my own association with the lecture series may be relevant. I served as director of strategic planning in the Executive Office of the Secretary-General during the last six months of Kofi Annan's first term and the entire five years of his second term. One of my most pleasurable duties was organizing the lectures. This volume was born of the conviction that the lectures would be of general interest to those broadly concerned about the United Nations, global issues, and timeless questions.

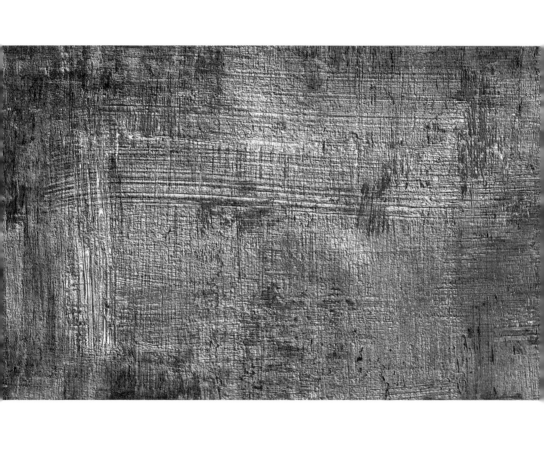

I.

Literature and Music

1

The Humanities after 9/11

TONI MORRISON

I am hoping you will agree that the piece of literature I want to draw from is, as its translator says, equal to our knowledge of reality in the present time, and discover, as I have done, in the lines of association which I am making with the medieval sensibility and a modern one, both of which turn out to be fertile ground on which we can appraise our contemporary world.

I am going to tell you a story, first, because narrative is probably the most effective way knowledge is structured and, second, because I am a storyteller, and the practice of writing makes demands on me that nothing else does.

The search for language, whether among other writers or in the process of writing, constitutes a mission. Delving into literature is neither an escape nor a surefire route to comfort. It has been a constant, sometimes violent, always provocative engagement with the contemporary world, the issues of the society we live in.

So, you will not be surprised that I take my text from ancient, but by no means remote, sources. The story is this. As I tell it, you may be reminded of the events and rhetoric and actions of many current militarized struggles and violent upheavals.

Once upon a time, there lived a man-eating monster of unprecedented cruelty and unparalleled appetite who ravaged generally at night and focused primarily on the people of one particular kingdom, but it was only because he chose to. Clearly, he could slaughter whomever and wherever he decided to. His name was Grendel and he spent a dozen years dismembering, chewing, and swallowing the livestock, the things, and the citizens of Scandinavia.

The leader of the besieged country lived at a great mead-hall with his queen, his family, friends, guards, counsels, and a grand army of heroes. Each night, when the leader retired, guards and warriors were stationed to protect the hall and its inhabitants from destruction, and to try to slay, if at all possible, their nighttime enemy. And each night, Grendel picked them off as though they were ripe cherries on an eternally fruited tree.

The kingdom was sunk in mourning and helplessness, riven with sorrow for the dead, with regret for the past, and in fear of the future. They were in the same situation as the Finns of one of their sagas: "Hooped within the great seal of necessity, in thrall to a code of loyalty and bravery, bound to seek glory in the eye of the warrior's world. The little nations are grouped around their lord, the greater nations spoil for war and menace the little ones, a lord dies, defenselessness ensues, the enemy strikes; vengeance for the dead becomes an ethic for the living, bloodshed begets further bloodshed, the wheel turns, the generations tread, and tread, and tread."

But what seemed never to trouble or worry them was who was Grendel and why had he placed them on his menu. Nowhere in the story is that question put. The question does not surface for a simple reason. Evil has no father. It is preternatural and exists without explanation.

Grendel's actions are dictated by his nature, the nature of an alien mind and inhuman drift. He is the essence of the one who loathes you, wants you not just dead, but nourishingly so, so that your death provides game to the slayer, food, land, wealth, water, whatever, like genocide, ethnic cleansing, mass murder, or individual assault for profit.

But Grendel escapes these reasons. No one had attacked or offended him. No one had tried to invade his home or displace him from his territory. No one had stolen from him or visited any wrath upon him.

Obviously, he was neither defending himself nor seeking vengeance. In fact, no one knew who he was.

He was not angry with the Danes. He did not want to rule their land or plunder their resources or rape their women. So, there could be no reasoning with him, no bribery, no negotiations, no begging. No trading could stop him.

Humans, even at their most corrupt, selfish, and ignorant, can be made available to reason, are educable, retrainable, and, most important, fathomable. Humans have words for madness, explanations for evil, and a system of payback for those who trespass or are judged outlaws.

But Grendel was beyond comprehension, unfathomable, the ultimate monster, mindless, without intelligible speech. In the illustrations and pictures that imagine him, and in the language that describe him, Grendel is ugly, hairy. His body is folded in on itself, breaking, easy, and most comfortable on all fours.

But even without claws, rows of shark-like teeth, even if he had been beautiful, it would not have lessened the horror. His mere presence in the world was an affront to it.

Eventually, of course, a brave and fit hero named Beowulf volunteers to rid the kingdom of this pestilence. He and his task force of warriors enter the land, announce their purpose, and are welcomed with enthusiasm and generosity.

On the very first night, following a celebration to rally the forces and draw their courage, the war is won. Or so it seemed. When the monster appears, they suffer only one casualty before Beowulf rips off Grendel's arm, sending him fatally bleeding, limping, moaning, slouching back home to his mother.

Yes, mother. I suggested earlier that evil has no father, but it should not come as a surprise that Grendel has a mother. In true folkloric, epic fashion, the bearer of evil, of destruction, is female. Monsters, it seems, are born after all.

And, like her sisters Eve, Pandora, Lot's wife, Helen of Troy, and the female that sits at the gate of Milton's hell birthing vicious dogs who eat each other and are replaced by more and more litters from their mother's womb, it turns out that Grendel's mother is more repulsive, more responsible for evil than he is.

Interestingly enough, she has no name and cannot speak. In any case, this silent, repulsive female is a mother and, unlike her child, does have a motive for murder. Therefore, she sets out immediately to avenge her dead son.

She advances to the mead-hall, interrupts the warriors reveling at their victory, and fills the pouch she carries with their mangled bodies. I rather like the idea of her with a pocketbook, which the translator calls a pouch.

Her vengeance instigates a second, even more determined foray by Beowulf, this time on the monster's territory and in his home. Beowulf swims through demon-laden waters, is captured, and entering the mother's lair weaponless, is forced to use his bare hands. He fights mightily, but unsuccessfully until suddenly, and fortunately, he grabs a sword that belongs to the mother. With this, her own weapon, he cuts off her head, and then the head of Grendel's corpse.

A curious thing happens then. The victim's blood melts the sword. The conventional reading is that the fiend's blood is so foul it melts steel, but the image of Beowulf standing there with a woman's head in one hand and a useless hilt in the other encourages more and layered interpretations, one being that perhaps violence against violence, regardless of good and evil, right and wrong, is itself so foul that the sword of vengeance collapses in exhaustion.

Beowulf is a classic epic of good vanquishing evil, of unimaginable brutality being overcome by physical force, bravery, sacrifice, honor, pride, rewards, both in reputations and wealth. All come full circle in this rousing medieval tale.

In such heroic narratives, glory is not in the details. The forces of good and evil are obvious, blatant. The triumph of the former over the latter is earned, justified, and delicious. As Beowulf says, "It is always better to avenge dear ones than to indulge in mourning. So arise, my lord, and let us immediately set forth on the trail of this troll-dam. I guarantee you: she will not get away, not to dens underground nor upland groves nor the ocean floor. She'll have nowhere to flee to."

Contemporary society, however, is made uneasy by the concept of pure, unmotivated evil, and by pious, unsullied virtue, and contemporary writers and scholars search for more. One challenge to the necessary, but narrow expectations of this heroic narrative comes from a contemporary writer, the late John Gardner in his novel titled *Grendel*. Told from the monster's point of view, it is tour de force and an intellectual and aesthetic enterprise that comes very close to being the sotto voce subject of much of today's efforts to come to grips with the kind of permanent global war we now seem to find ourselves engaged in.

The novel poses the question that the epic does not: who is Grendel? The author asks us to enter his mind and test the assumption that evil is flagrantly unintelligible, wanton, and undecipherable. By assuming Grendel's voice, his point of view, Gardner establishes at once that, unlike the character in the poem, Grendel is not without thought and is not a beast. In fact, he is reflecting precisely on true beasts the moment the reader is introduced to him. When the novel opens, he is watching a ram, musing, "Do not think my brains are squeezed shut like a ram's by the roots of horns." And further, "Why can't these creatures discover a little dignity?"

Gardner's version has the same plot, characters, and so forth as the original and relies on similar descriptions and conventions: referring to women, for example, only queens have names. If Grendel's mother has a name, it is as unspeakable as she is unspeaking. But where Seamus Heaney's introduction to his translation emphasizes the movement of evil from out there to in here, from the margins to the world to inside the castle in the artistic brilliance of the poem, the beautiful contrivances of its language, Gardner, on the other hand, tries to penetrate the interior life—emotional, cognizant of incarnate evil—and prioritizes the poet as one who organizes the world's disorder, who pulls together disparate histories into meaning.

We learn in Gardner's novel that Grendel distinguishes himself from the ram that does not know or remember his past. We learn that Grendel in the beginning is consumed by hatred and is neither proud nor ashamed of it, that he is full of contempt for the survivors of his rampages.

Watching the human things bury their dead, he describes the scenes: "On the side of the hill, the dirge-slow shoveling begins. They throw up a mound for the funeral pyre, for whatever arms or legs or heads my haste has left behind. Meanwhile, up in the shattered hall, the builders are hammering, replacing the door, industrious and witless as worker ants—except that they make small, foolish changes, adding a few more iron pegs, more iron bands, with tireless dogmatism." Grendel's contempt extends to the world in general: "I understood that the world was nothing: a mechanical chaos of casual, brute enmity on which we stupidly impose our hopes and fears. I understand that, finally and absolutely, I alone exist. All the rest, I saw, is merely what pushes me, or what I push against, blindly—as blindly as all that is not myself pushes back. I create the whole universe, blink by blink."

But the fundamental theme of the novel lies in Grendel's possibilities. First, his encounter with shaped, studied, artistic language, as opposed to noise, groans, shouts, and boasts. And, second, his dialogue with the dragon who sits atop the mountain of gold he has been guarding for centuries.

Regarding the first, his encounter with the poet called the Shaper offers him the only possibility of transformation. Grendel knows that the Shaper's song is full of lies, of illusion. He has watched carefully the battles of men and knows that they are not the glory the singer turns them into. But he succumbs to the Shaper's language nevertheless, because of its power to transform, its power to elevate, to discourage base action. He defines the poet's potency this way: "He reshapes the world, so his name implies. He stares strange-eyed at the mindless world and turns dry sticks to gold."

It is because of this shaped, elevated, patterned language that Grendel is able to contemplate beauty, recognize love, feel pity, crave mercy, and experience shame. It is because of the Shaper's imagination that he considers the equation of quality with meaning. In short, he develops a desperate hunger for the life of a completely human being.

"My heart," he says, "was light with Hrothgar's goodness, and leaden with grief at my own bloodthirsty ways." Overwhelmed with these reflections on goodness and light, he goes to the mead-hall weeping for mercy, aching for community to assuage his utter loneliness.

"I staggered out into the open and up toward the hall with my burden, groaning out mercy, peace. The Shaper broke off, the people screamed, drunken men rushed to me with battleaxes. I sank to my knees crying, 'Friend, friend.' They hacked at me, yipping like dogs."

So he reverts to the deep wilderness of his hatred. Yet he is still in turmoil, torn between tears and a bellow of scorn. He travels to the dragon for answers to his own cosmic questions: Why am I here? What is God? What is the world?

At the end of a long and fascinating argument, loaded with the dragon's cynicism, bitterness, indifference, Grendel receives one piece of advice from the dragon: get a pile of gold and sit on it.

Grendel's noble language produces noble behavior, just as empty language produces empty behavior, and the dragon's view of man's stupidity, banality, and irrelevance, his denial of freewill and intercession right there, exactly there, lays the plane on which civic and intellectual life rests, rocks, and rolls.

Grendel's dilemma is also ours. It is the nexus between the Shaper and the dragon, between St. Augustine and Nietzsche, between art and science, between the Old Testament and the New, between swords and plowshares.

It is the space for, as well as the act of, thought. It is a magnetic space, pulling us away from reaction to thinking, denying easy answers and violence committed because in crisis it is the only thing one knows how to do.

The language of war has historically been noble, summoning the elevating quality of warrior discourse, the eloquence of grief for the dead, courage, and the honor of vengeance. That heroic language rendered by Homer, by Shakespeare, in sagas, and by statesmen is rivaled for beauty and force only by religious language with which it frequently merges.

In this parade of inspiring war talk, from BC to the twentieth century there have been disruptions. One moment of distrust and disdain for such language occurred immediately after World War I, when writers like Ernest Hemingway, Wilfred Owen, among others, questioned the paucity of such terms as honor, glory, bravery, courage to describe the reality of war, the obscenity of those terms being associated with the carnage of 1914 through 1918.

Hemingway wrote, "I was always embarrassed by the words sacred, glorious, and sacrifice and the expression in vain. We had heard them sometimes standing in the rain almost out of earshot, and I would see nothing sacred, and the things that were glorious had no glory, and the sacrifices were like the stockyards at Chicago if nothing was done with the meat except to bury it. There were many names you could not bear to hear, and finally, only the names of places had dignity."

But the events of 1938 quieted those interventions, and once more the language of war rose to the occasion of World War II. The glamor-coated images we carry of Roosevelt, Churchill, and other statesmen are due in part to their rousing speeches and are testimony to the strength of militant oratory.

Yet something interesting happened after World War II. In the late fifties and sixties, wars continued, of course, hot, cold, north, south, big, small, more and more cataclysmic, more and more heartbreaking because so unnecessary, so wildly punitive on innocent civilians, one could only drop to one's knees in sorrow.

Yet the language that accompanied these recent wars became oddly diminished. The dwindling persuasiveness of combat discourse may have been due to the low requirements of commercial media, their abhorrence of complex sentences and less-known metaphors, the dominance of the visual over linguistic communication. Or perhaps it was due to the fact that all of these wars were the seething, mute children of preceding ones. Whatever the cause, warrior discourse has become childlike, puny, vaguely prepubescent. Underneath the speeches, bulletins, punditry, essays lies the clear whine of the playground. "He hit me." "I did not." "Did too." "That's mine." "Is not." "Is too." "I hate you." "I hate you."

This decline, it seems to me, this echo of passionate juvenilia affects the highest level of contemporary warrior discourse and sounds like that of the comic book or action film. "I strike for freedom." "We must save the world." "Houston, we have a problem."

An inane, enfeeble screed has emerged to address brain-cracking political and economic problems. What is fascinating is that such language sank to its plodding at precisely the time another language was evolving, the language of nonviolence, of peaceful resistance, of negotiation, the language of Gandhi, of Martin Luther King, of Nelson Mandela, of Vaclav Havel, compelling language, robust, subtle, elevating, intelligent, complex.

As war's consequences became more and more dire, war talk has become less and less credible, more infantile in its panic. A change became obvious just at the moment when the language of resolution, of diplomacy, was developing its own idiom, a moral idiom worthy of human intelligence, shedding the cloud of weakness, of appeasement that historically has hovered above it.

I do not believe the shift is coincidental. I believe it represents a fundamental change in the concept of war, a not-so-secret conviction among various and sundry populations, both oppressed and privileged, that war is finally out of date, that it is truly the most inefficient method of achieving one's long-term aims.

No matter the paid parades, the forced applause, the instigated riots, the organized protests, pro or con, self- or state censoring, the propaganda, no matter the huge opportunities for profited gain, and no matter the history of the injustice. At bottom, it is impossible to escape the suspicion that the more sophisticated the weapons of war, the more antiquated the idea of war; the more transparent the power grab, the holier the justification; the more arrogant the claims, the more barbaric, the more discredited the language of war has become.

Leaders who find war the sole and inevitable solution to disagreement, displacement, aggression, injustice, and abasing poverty seem not only helplessly retrograde but also intellectually deficient, precisely like the empurpled comic book language in which they express themselves.

I understand that my comments may appear disjunctive on this date in 2002, when legislatures, revolutionaries, and the inflamed do not declare war, but simply wage it. But I am convinced that the language that has the most force, that requires the more acumen, talent, grace, genius, and, yes, beauty, can never be, will never again be, found in paeans to the glory of war or erotic rallying cries to battle.

The power of this alternative language does not arise from the tiresome, wasteful art of war, but, rather, from the demanding, brilliant art of peace.

2

The Use of Language in War and Peace

CHINUA ACHEBE AND PAUL MULDOON

Chinua Achebe

In 1972 I received my first honorary doctor of letters degree. It came to me all the way from Dartmouth College in New Hampshire to my war-ravaged hideout in Nigeria. The only thing I was to do in return for becoming a doctor was to give a public lecture on the eve of commencement. No topic or title was pressed on me or even suggested. I was young and serious-minded in those days and decided on the grand topic of language and the destiny of man.

I am not as bold today as I was then, and I am grateful to Secretary-General Kofi Annan, who leads this great shrine of peace and cooperation among nations, for giving me this honor to speak here on a subject of truly monumental relevance, a subject on which our life depends, for making it simple by proposing a topic, and, further, having two people to look at it, because my people have a proverb that says two heads, four eyes.

In 1972 it was not difficult for me to be thinking and talking about human survival. I had just been through a horrendous civil war, one of the worst of the twentieth century, a war that first brought into people's living rooms around the world appalling images of starving children on evening television.

Today nothing much seems to have changed. It may not be Biafra and Nigeria, but instead Darfur and Sudan and many other places where human survival is not a theoretical issue.

I would like to quote a short passage from my Dartmouth College address, after which I promise to say nothing more about what I did in 1972: "Speech, like society itself, seems so natural that we rarely give much thought to it or contemplate man's circumstance before its invention, but we know that language is not inherent in man. The capacity for language, yes, but not language. Therefore, there must have been a time in the very distant past when our ancestors did not have language."

Let us imagine a very simple incident in those days. A man strays into a rock shelter without knowing that another is already there, finishing a meal in the dark interior. The first hint a newcomer gets of this fact is a piece of rock hurled at his head.

In a different kind of situation —which we shall call, with guilty reservations, human—in a human situation, that confrontation might have been resolved less catastrophically by the simple question "What do you want?" or even an angry "Get out of here!"

Nobody is going to be so naive as to suggest that language is a panacea for every conflict and violence, but it may have a small chance of slowing down a rush to war. In other words, language may offer a chance to fight tomorrow instead of today, which is not a lot of chance or promise. Anyone who says it is nothing is yet to experience war.

My people sometimes reveal a weird sense of humor about themselves. They will tell you, for example, that if a man commits the most egregious, the most abominable, offense and no one immediately jumps up and cuts off his head, the next thing you will hear is, "How are we going to deal with this? What are we going to do now?" That question is like a small chink that lets humanity's shaky voice into the stunning silence of a fearful retribution.

The ability of language to mediate in human conflict depends on the trust we can place in the words we hear and in the person speaking them. The integrity of language is stronger than the value of any currency. Whenever we use language fraudulently or even just callously, we undermine the basis of human communication, which is weak and fragile to begin with.

When I came to this country in the early 1970s for my first extended stay, I did not notice that the word *aggressive* was a good word. I did not notice that people were expected to do things aggressively. I spent four years teaching in Massachusetts and Connecticut and then went back to Nigeria in blissful ignorance that it was good to be aggressive.

Two decades later, I returned to America on my current visit. I could not believe my ears. The *A* word was flying and buzzing all around me, culminating in the classic exchange between an American journalist and Hans Blix, the Swedish leader of the United Nations Monitoring, Verification, and Inspection Commission (UNMOVIC), looking for weapons of mass destruction in Iraq. The journalist was accusing Mr. Blix and his team of failing to look aggressively for the weapons, whereupon the Swede made a refined joke about the United Nations' charter prohibition on aggression—a joke the journalist missed entirely.

I began this talk suggesting that language could be called humanity's defense against violence and war, but we must recognize language's capacity to also become a problem instead of a solution. The reason is that language is as complex as the human mind that fashioned it.

Language may use simple, direct statements, or instead ambiguity and metaphor. I do not know when we began to use war as a metaphor for sustained opposition to things we disapprove of or things we are expected to approve of. In Nigeria, one of our military regimes even declared war against indiscipline. WAI, it was called. This declaration required city dwellers to join their neighbors in cleaning up garbage in the environment every other Saturday.

The good thing about a metaphor is that everyone knows it is make-believe. However close it might get to fact, we know it is not true literally, which was why some of us in Nigeria found the conscription-style war on indiscipline somewhat troubling. Our anxiety came from knowing that our soldiers were not particularly trained in the use of metaphor.

What about war on terrorism? What about America? As in every other matter, America sets the pace today for the rest of the world. 9/11 was a watershed event for checking the relationship between war and language. Because what happened that day was a huge, unprecedented, unimagined subversion of the promises of technology by a backward, vengeful barbarity, language was captured and taken hostage by war.

Overnight, war as metaphor, as literary make-believe, was discharged and replaced by hardware reality, by actual troops invading an actual country. Perhaps we should never have thought that something as deadly as war could be used in play. Perhaps any war game is doomed to end as war. Perhaps this is a time to review other metaphors, like war on poverty or war on disease, lest we wake up one morning and find that somebody somewhere is dropping bombs on poor people and sick people.

A discussion of the use of language in war and peace ends up, I am afraid, talking a lot about war and very little about peace. Sadly, that seems to be the human condition, or at least the condition of our world today.

Peace is fragile. It cannot survive the unruliness of the rough house. Mere words can kill peace.

The people of my village tell us that he who would forbid war must first banish the raising of voices and the wagging of the finger in the face. That is why the United Nations was founded, to intervene in quarrels among nations when they are still only fiery speech and threatening gestures. Yet this day we find in certain quarters people who are ready to belittle the UN and its mission to anticipate trouble in the world and work to stop or minimize it through careful and sensitive use of language. We have our work cut out for us.

Paul Muldoon

One of the tyrannies of the alphabet is that I must follow Secretary-General Annan and Chinua Achebe. I want to say a word or two about how difficult it is to come directly after them, how difficult it is to follow hard on their heels, and what a tall order that might be.

I want to look at a couple of those words, picking up on what we were hearing about the aggressive search for weapons of mass destruction. The words I want to focus on to begin with are *tall*, tall in the sense of the small drink we order in the coffee store and in which we collude, knowing that it is a small drink—we collude in the notion that it is a tall drink.

The other word I want to focus on for a moment is the word *direct*, if I may be direct with you. If you take a direct flight in this day and age, one is more likely than not to stop somewhere along the way. We accept this as being how language functions. We accept this as being appropriate.

We can figure out, I think, that this is an instance of language being used as a tool. I want to say a word or two about language as a tool.

That, indeed, is a notion which has inspired many artists. The notion of the poet, for example, is that of the maker in Greek. As you know, the basis of that word *poem* or *poet* has to do with a construct in the world, something that is made in the world. The poet is the maker. So the poem as a construct written by someone who is using language as tool is a significant component. There is also another idea of poetry, and that is the poem as a found object, which occurs in, say, the French and Italian traditions of the troubadour, the person who stumbles upon the work of art and who, if anything, is used as a tool by the language.

It is that aspect of our relationship, both in war and peace, with the language that I would like to pursue today, because what I am talking about is the idea that we be humble before the language. Rather than going into any circumstance with a sense of what the appropriate thing to say might be, to go into it in a spirit of humility, which is, as far as I can see, one of the defining characteristics of any great artist, that he or she is humble before the possibility of art.

We can move on from art to other human circumstances, but basically it is right to go through the world with the notion that Wordsworth described as wise passiveness or that Keats described as negative capability. That is to say, the ability which Keats recognized in Shakespeare in particular, if you recall, of being content not to go after irritable fact and reason but to go, as he says, by uncertainties, mysteries, to go in the spirit that the great German philosopher Eugen Herrigel went to Japan to study with a master archer, an archer who could, if you know this book, *Zen and the Art of Archery*, who could hit a bullseye blindfolded, who could hit it in the dead of night. How on earth could he manage such a thing? Only when he accepted that he had nothing to do with it, only when he accepted that it shoots, it hits.

So what I want to do now before we open up the conversation, which I think is part of our plan here this afternoon, is to read a bit of a poem, if you don't mind, a little Exhibit A, as it were. It's a poem set in a country which I think may be partly Ireland but not wholly Ireland. It's called The Old Country, which would suggest that it might have something to do with Ireland, but not absolutely exclusively, I think, because it's a country in which, like almost all these days, there is a likelihood that language may not exactly correspond, a word may not entirely correspond, with what it's meant to be describing. There may be some little discrepancy between tall and tall and between direct and direct.

This is a sonnet sequence. The very thought makes one tremble, I know, but I'm going to read a few pieces of it. I think you'll get the idea. You may, in fact, join in. You would be very welcome, because one of the things that is happening here is that it is a poem that involves itself in platitudes, I suppose by way of hoping to stave them off.

So, The Old Country:

Where every town was a tidy town
and every garden a hanging garden,
A half—that's a half of whiskey—could be had for half a crown.
Every major artery would harden
since every meal was a square meal.
Every clothesline showed a line of undies
yet no house was in dishabille.

Every Sunday took a month of Sundays
til everyone got it off by heart.
Every start was a bad start
since all conclusions were foregone.

Every wood had its twist of woodbine.
Every cliff its herd of fatalistic swine.
Every runnel was a Rubicon
and every annual a hardy annual
applying itself like linen to the lawn.
Every glove compartment held a manual
and a map of the roads, major and minor.
Every major road had major road works.
Every wishy-washy water diviner
had stood like a bulwark
against something worth standing against.

The smell of incense left us incensed
at the firing of the fort.

Every heron was a presager
of some disaster after which, we'd wager,

every resort was a last resort.
Every resort was a last resort
with a harbor that harbored an old grudge.

Every sale was a selling short.
There were those who simply wouldn't budge
from the Dandy to the Rover.

That shouting was the shouting
but for which it was all over the weekend, I mean, we set off an outing
with the weekday train timetable.

Every tower was a Tower of Babel
that graced each corner of a bawn
where every lookout was a poor lookout.
Every rill had its unflashy trout.
Every runnel was a Rubicon.

Are you getting the idea? One of the terrible problems with this poem—I'm sure there are many problems, but one of them is that it became much too much fun to write, which is surely an indicator that something is going awry.

Every runnel was a Rubicon
where every ditch was a last ditch.
Every man was "a grand wee mon"
whose every pitch was another sales pitch
now every boat was a burned boat.
Every cap was a cap in hand.
Every coat a trailed coat.
Every band was a gallant band
across the broken bridge
and broken ridge after broken ridge
where you couldn't beat a stick with a big stick.

Every straight road was a straightup speed trap.
Every decision was a snap.
Every cut was a cut to the quick.

Every cut was a cut to the quick.
when the weasel's twist met the weasel's tooth
and Christ was somewhat impolitic
in branding as "weasels fighting in a hole," forsooth
the petrol-smugglers back on the old sod
when a vender of red diesel
for whom every rod was a green rod
reminded one and all that the weasel
was nowhere to be found in that same quarter.

No mere mortal could withstand a ten-inch mortar.
Every hope was a forlorn hope.

So it was that the defenders
were taken in by their own blood-splendor.
Every slope was a slippery slope.

Every slope was a slippery slope
where every shave was a very close shave
and money was money for old rope,
where every grave was a watery grave
now every boat was, again, a burned boat.
Every dime-a-dozen rat, a dime-a-dozen drowned rat
except for the whitrack or stoat,
which the very Norsemen had down pat
as a weasel-word
though we know their speech was rather slurred.
Every time was time in the nick
just as every nick was a nick in time.
Every unsheathed sword was somehow sheathed in rime.
Every cut was a cut to the quick.
Every cut was a cut to the quick,
what with every feather a feather to ruffle.

Every whitrack was a whitterick.
Everyone was in a right kerfuffle
when from his hob some hobbledehoy
would venture the whitterick was a curlew.

I hope the translators are making some sense of this. I have to say that even for me it's a bit of a problem. So my sincere apologies to you.

> Every wall was a wall of Troy
> and every hunt a hunt in the purlieu
> of a demesne so out of bounds
> every hound might have been a hell-hound.
> At every lane-end stood a milk-churn
> whose every dent was a sign of indenture
> to some pig-wormer or cattle-drencher.
> Every point was a point of no return.

I think I'll skip through one or two of them, if you don't mind, be-cause really—yes, I mean part of the point of this—insofar as it is a poem—is that it's mimetic of the very tedium that it's describing, and that is a problem, because we don't like to associate tedium and art.

> Every track was an inside track
> where every horse had the horse sense
> to know it was only a glorified hack.

> Every graineen of gratitude was immense
> and every platitude a familiar platitude.
> Every kemple of hay was a kemple tossed in the air
> by a haymaker in a hay-feud.
> Every chair at the barn dance a musical chair
> given how every paltry poltroon
> and his paltry dog could carry a tune
> yet no one would carry the can
> any more than Sampson would carry the temple.

> Every spinal column was a collapsing stemple.
> Every flash was a flash in the pan.
> Every flash was a flash in the pan
> and every border a herbaceous border
> unless it happened to be an
> herbaceous border as observed by the Recorder
> or recorded by the Observer.

Every widdie stemmed from a willow-bole.
Every fervor was a religious fervor
by which we'd fly the godforsaken hole
into which we'd been flung by it.

Every pit was a bottomless pit
out of which every pig needed a piggyback.

Biddy winked at Paddy, and Paddy winked at Biddy.
Every cow had subsided in its subsidy.
Every track was an inside track.

Every track was an inside track,
and every job and inside job.

Every whitterick had been a whitrack
until, from his hobbledehob,
that hobbledehobbledehoy had insisted the whitterick was a curlew.

But every boy was still "one of the boys"
and every girl your "ye girl ye"
for whom every dance was a last dance
and every chance a last chance
and every let-down a terrible let-down

from the days when every list was a laundry list
in that old country where, we reminisced,
every town was a tidy town.

So I offer that as an example of what can go seriously wrong.

3

Why Music Matters?

LEON BOTSTEIN

Thank you, Mr. Secretary-General, for the kind invitation. And I thank all of you for coming out to this talk. It is humbling for any private citizen to address this organization the UN. This is particularly so for an American. We as a nation are the hosts of the UN, yet we have not always been its staunchest defenders or most vigorous admirers. One of the privileges of being an American is the right to dissent, particularly in these times, so there are many of us who would like to see the day when the promise of the UN is realized with American cooperation and enthusiasm.

Early in its history, the United Nations inspired a few composers. In 1949, the American, Aaron Copland, wrote his *Preamble for a Solemn Occasion*. It was performed here, with Laurence Olivier narrating and Leonard Bernstein conducting. Copland used the words of the United Nations Charter, about half of its preamble, to honor the first anniversary of the Universal Declaration of Human Rights. The style of the work was prophetic, rhetorical, and imposing: befitting, as some noted, the voice of an Old Testament prophet. Copland sought to use music to preach an ideal that in 1949 had become clouded by domestic reactions against communism, the Cold War, and fear of atomic war. The world was free of Hitler but not of Stalin; nor of the legacy of nineteenth-century colonialism. Ethnic strife in India, religious conflict in the Middle East, and war in Indochina were all grim realities.

I cite this example because, while we would like to think and believe that music matters, explaining why is not easy. For in truth, if "mattering" is measured by the harmony, beauty, peace, tranquility, tolerance, and understanding it generates, music no more than language has mattered in the practical utilitarian sense. However, there is no evidence that music has made us more civil, more peaceful, or more respectful, or helped make the world safer and more livable. Copland's use of music with the text of the Preamble had no impact. Now, one can say, "Well, maybe it wasn't a very good work." But on the same program was the most famous piece of western music that explicitly tries to use music to create human solidarity—the Ninth Symphony of Beethoven. Yet it too has not brought us more peace and harmony. It was used to celebrate the fall of the Berlin Wall. It was used to celebrate Hitler's birthday in 1941.

Consider, for example, Mozart. Stalin loved Mozart. That taste, refined as it is, did not rein in his capacity for brutality. My own grandfather recalled hiding in a closet in the Warsaw ghetto where, like him, others were desperately trying to elude capture, particularly mothers with children, knowing that the result of discovery was deportation to Auschwitz. The SS officer in charge of that raid noticed a piano in the room, a rarity in the ghetto. While people were hiding, and after having sent dozens to death, he sat down and played, with an angelic look, gloriously the music of Schumann, Chopin, and Mozart.

Elias Canetti, the Nobel laureate, once wrote that one of the most terrifying clichés we repeat and the cruelest is that language fosters communication. Next in line should probably be music, that it is universal and can actually cross divides of class, religion, and nationality. Consider the case of language. We all have the capacity for language. It defines a unique aspect of our common humanity. So it is with music, which in its many forms might be inherent to us all. Though we all speak and translate, neither in public nor in private does language itself, notwithstanding its universality and our capacity to identify common elements of syntax, grammar, semantics, and rhetoric, necessarily create peace and harmony. If speech is action, and if debate, dialogue and negotiation, not violence, is the primary instrument of politics, then language can matter if we can agree, in speech, on shared meanings, rules, and procedures. At stake, therefore, is not language per se, but a particular language or particular languages used in particular ways, with agreed-upon goals and correspondences between meanings and words. Reaching this human agreement worldwide on such principles has not yet been successful.

Sustaining a shared discourse has become difficult even in our own country, the United States, where words and notions of law, procedures, and rights have ceased to reveal shared principles and agreements. We now find language used as euphemism, slogans and jargons on all sides, that make it harder and harder to use language to achieve clarity and understanding. But our founders believed that language could be used to foster human understanding and that it mattered.

Indeed, music may not matter, if we speak only of music as a universal phenomenon in the ordinary sense. There are two forms of music that are nearly ubiquitous. John Blacking, the eminent social anthropologist—who spent most of his career thinking, teaching, and writing about music at Queen's University, ironically in Belfast, a locus classicus of how difficult it is, despite a common language, to promote human understanding—made the point emphatically through empirical research that music was a universal characteristic of all human beings, a "form of life" as the philosopher Ludwig Wittgenstein once put it. Blacking did field work not in Europe, but in South Africa, among the Venda.

What Blacking defined as music was the universal creation of pitch structures, rhythmic patterns, and rules by which these can be changed, organized, and adapted into units of sound that all humans create in acoustic, artificial space—a realm in which they organize sounds that are not found in nature over time, and these modes of organization alter their sense of time. We experience time through music differently from the way we experience time in the clock or by the sun and natural phenomenon, and we develop an internal sensibility of time through music. This universal impulse and cognitive capacity that Blacking found inherent engages the participation of everyone. There's no one unmusical by this logic. The specific ways we organize sound, the way we create pitch and use music, however, is defined by communities, and like language, differs as you travel place to place.

This form of universal music is what in the nineteenth century came to be called folk music, and there is no human community without it. The Hungarian composer Béla Bartók studied and documented this tradition in the early 1900s. He went to premodern rural areas in modern-day Hungary, Slovakia, Romania, and Moldova. Traveling later in his career to northern Africa, he concluded that all folk music has something in common in its pitch structure and rhythmic patterns, and they are all interrelated.

Bartók, by the mid-1930s an avowed anti-Fascist, was determined to prove fraudulent the use of folk music to justify chauvinism and individious national distinctions. He infuriated right-wing Hungarians, still angry at the Treaty of Trianon, that "their" authentic folk music was no different than and was perhaps derived from Romanian and Slovakian folk patterns. And they were all offended at the notion that it might have come from Africa.

In contrast, the Czech, or rather Moravian, composer Leoš Janáček wanted to find a different argument for the distinctly national quality of folk music by creating in his own music sounds that related to the specific character of the Czech language, what he called speech melodies, so he could find a way to defend the natural impulse for music through the distinct nature of a particular language.

This folk tradition we would call spontaneous, some of it premodern, has indeed found its modern mirror image in the second most powerful universal aspect of music, popular commercial music. This is a comparatively recent phenomenon. It's an example of early globalization. With the introduction of a stable and easily distributable means of reproduction of music in Europe and North America—first the piano, then the radio and gramophone, and now the iPod and CD—there is a new international style, part white American, part African American, part Latin American, African, and European. This mélange has emerged in dance, popular music, Muzak in airports, and urban street music, and there is in it, unfortunately, the perception of a kind of Americanization.

This has troubled many nationalists. Just as Esperanto died a natural death only to cede to English the role of a potential international language, resistance to this perceived loss of authentic local culture is great, whether in Europe or in Iran. In music, the enemies of popular commercial culture see a sort of global standardization, a musical Mc-Donalds or Coca-Cola effect, by which people with access to the communication systems of modernity acquire by imitation surrogates to the real experience of making music. They buy things the way they would food or clothing, and the standardization seems at odds with the purpose and importance of music. Everything is identically packaged. However, as the music is heard, it is made and appropriated by the individual, and each individual finds its meaning in it, even though they sometimes discover that their personal meaning seems quite similar, one to the next.

Were this power of universality of commercial music a force for enlightenment and even progress, it would create more than the older traditions of social folk music and more passive listeners. The fact remains that despite the commonality of this appropriation of music, it seems that we do not have a way to use this common purchase of music as a basis for new human understanding. But the spread of popular music should not be derided, either. That is, the criticism of popular music as somehow being morally wrong or morally troubling seems nonsensical. The music is of limited duration; it depends on words and is subject to rapid shifts in fashion. Music matters here primarily as commerce, entertainment—and requires very little active engagement beyond perhaps karaoke and dancing.

Now, this does not mean that there are not great, better and lesser, and poor examples of popular music: the observation about commercial music is not an aesthetic judgment. It is very hard to write good music in any genre; there's genius in every field. But as to the question of whether music matters in terms of ethics and politics, and bettering the human condition, neither folk nor commercial music do the task we expect of it.

So the question then becomes: Is there a form of music, a way of using music the way we might use the language that in fact does create the possibility for more universal understanding? In each civilization—in the West, in India, in China—just as in speech and language, humans have developed a counterintuitive dimension of music. That counterintuitive dimension goes beyond the evident and the natural. Much like science and mathematics, this music often contradicts what we think of as true. For example, the earth is not flat, and objects of different masses fall at the same rate. The earth revolves around the sun, not the other way around. And, as our DNA shown, we are more similar than we are different, despite our notions of race or our obsessions with the geometry of a face.

The world of science and mathematics is often arcane and seemingly abstract. In the case of mathematics, the questions and answers often have no practical application. In music in all cultures, systems of making music over long stretches of time, discretely and completely independent of words and pictures, lasting minutes, hours, and in cases days, using the human voice, the gamelan, or the Western orchestra have extended the complexity of musical expectations, syntax, and semantics. Indeed, it is this—what we might call art music—that actually creates a world that we could not imagine, a new kind of experience that has no practical purpose.

It is a world that has mystery and that is entirely unpredictable. It is not only complex and sophisticated, but it also has the capacity of being, as in literature and art, simple. And one of the reasons it is so alluring is that in its simplicity and complexity, its innate contradiction, it has no fixed meaning. This music has no truth value. You can never, it can never, be judged as being right or wrong. It is utterly meaningless, in the ordinary sense of the world, and therefore it is hard to be appropriated.

What is important about this music, too, is that it is transferable. Composers can use this kind of music across barriers. Colin McFee did it with Indonesian music. Bright Sheng and Tan Dun do it to this day, matching the East and the West. There is no authenticity in this form of music. In recent decades, what we call Western classical music is enjoyed, played, and produced in Korea and Japan. We may deem it Western. It is not Western. It is their music. It has no stable meaning, cannot be owned, and permits no permanent national identification.

Now, this noncommercial, complex form of music—that is ephemeral and is performed and listened to at every moment of time differently—is something that is connected to the original folk and commercial tradition. The simple ideas that make the complex fabric of music often come from simple melodies. As Johannes Brahms, the composer, noted, Antonín Dvořák had the greatest talent for inventing melodies, and those melodies actually sounded like folk melodies, and that was the hardest thing to do in music.

What is very important about this form of music is that it is from the contemporary point of view often derided as being elitist, as being not accessible. But precisely because it is an opaque form of expression where meanings are unstable, it cannot be appropriated by any kind of power.

One of the great things about music and why it matters is that it is entirely imaginary and divorced from the everyday. It is boundless, unpredictable, untamable, and what stable meanings it has are contained in a particular moment. It gives one the sense that on one hand it is emotional and intense, and at the same time it is neutral. As its elusive humanity confronts us, it never repeats itself. There is in music a notion of repetition, in both Western music and notated music, but actually, because music follows time, no so-called repetition is actually a repeat. It is always a new event just as life never turns backwards in our experience. Finally, it has a connection to memory. Music creates an arena of memory that is insulated from political power and goes beyond the reach of language and image.

It is important to look at how music has functioned in this third, complex, imaginary, non-ordinary counterintuitive fashion—what we call art music. Under periods of dictatorship, it has been one of the few provinces of freedom protected from government and the willful use of power. In the period of Metternich's rule, after the fall of Napoleon, public performance of music was one of the few arenas where the public could gather without coming under suspicion, where people could show emotion and response without betraying so-called meaning in public that was within the reach of censorship. Under no torture or tyranny could an individual actually betray what they really meant. The meaningless, the lack of utility, the instability and yet the complexity of musical experience is its own protection in a period of un-freedom.

For those of us who live in relative freedom, where gathering in a public space is not a problem, music provides an opportunity for an irreducible individuality—the capacity for us to reinvent ourselves—in time, apart from the tyranny of the clock.

This august organization [the UN] was founded in the wake of one of the most terrifying experiences in recorded history, after people with education, cultivation, and learning engaged in the most rigorous barbarism. If we ever doubted the connections of education, cultivation, and ethics, it is the experience of the Second World War that teaches us that we, in fact, permitted ourselves, despite the advance of civilization, to lose the sense of the sanctity of human life.

Hannah Arendt in the early 1960s termed this the banality of evil. That banality now has become more directed to not only accepting that banality but also finding some entertainment value in a perverse way about it. This is seen as a relief from boredom, a sense of our own insignificance, powerlessness, a sense that life is not sacred.

Music may therefore be the last refuge of hope beyond language because it is in every human being; it is unpredictable and leads us to the boundless power of human imagination. It is a speechless form of life that can renew our respect and gratitude for my own life and the lives of others. It does not need to communicate over cultural lines. It simply needs to be, to have breath and life, and to permit each of us to discover that, as being musicians, we deserve the rights and the freedoms to which this organization is dedicated.

II.

Economics and
Human Rights

4

Globalization: Winners and Losers

JAGDISH BHAGWATI, JOSEPH STIGLITZ,
AND JEFFREY SACHS

The topic "globalization: winners and losers" is very appropriate, because the distribution issue is a question of justice, the quality of outcomes or equality of excess. Will globalization produce losers? Certainly it will. No economic process or policy proceeds like the Roman legion lock and step, with everybody moving at the same space—the people who take advantage of opportunities because they are richer or because they have more excess credit and so on. In every phenomenon you would be able to find some differential in the advance. Whether you have losers in the sense that people actually lose their shirt, become actually worse off, is something open to debate. But that there would be unequal advance, I think is inevitable.

Many developing countries have fallen behind. On the other hand, many developing countries, like India and China once they shifted to using the international system judiciously to take advantage of trade and investment, have produced rapid growth rates. Sometimes, economics and common sense do go together. If you grow more rapidly, you are more likely to be able to pull your masses of underemployed or unemployed people into gainful employment. If you look at both China and India, which, unfortunately, have enormous numbers of the poor, until the early 1980s, the growth rates were very limited. Since then, the growth rates have increased, due to a whole package of reforms, of which internationalization was a main element but not the only one. Globalization, at least on the trade front, led to favorable outcomes.

It is essential to be clear about which basic policy options you want to pursue. You have to decide whether you want to wear shoes or to go barefoot. Do you want to go for more integration in the world economy or do you want to turn backwards? We know that globalization, certainly in the sense of trade and multinational investment, is undoubtedly favorable for us, but certainly you will need to have the varying sizes adjusted for, depending on the country in question. Many countries decide to liberalize, but inevitably the pace at which they do it depends on domestic political and economic conditions. Inevitably countries are going to follow their own path regardless of what the World Bank or the IMF says.

I am pleased that the UN is promoting greater NGO participation around the world. In order to achieve development, both governments and NGOs must work together. NGOs can act as the eyes and ears of government policy. They also have a commitment not in the form of profit, but in terms of altruism and the environment. They can be, therefore, a partnership with the governments which have the money and the policies but not the knowledge with which to implement these things.

Globalization and economic development are both moving forward in the twenty-first century. These two great movements, globalization and civil society globalization, actually are very natural allies. We can look for I think what you call, Mr. Secretary-General, partnership, but I call it a shared success. It cannot be done by one party or the other. NGOs have knowledge and commitment but no funds, usually. Governments have funds and policies but no knowledge.

The issue is not whether to globalize. It is really how to shape it and how to make it work better and, for the developing countries, how to take advantage of it and to adapt to it. The way we shape globalization and the ability of developing countries to adapt to it will obviously affect the pace of globalization. It is important to recognize that globalization is not inevitably a one-way process, and there is a long history of globalization. In the area of economic globalization, there was more capital flows, trade, and movement of labor in the nineteenth century before World War I than there was during the interwar period. In many people's view, what happened in the interwar period represents a failure of global governance and that it has only been since World War II that globalization has begun again. But there are some very serious concerns about the way globalization has been managed and shaped.

Countries that have been most successful, especially in East Asia, have taken advantage of globalization, but have done so judiciously. The countries of East Asia, for instance, had their growth based on exports, which is a form of globalization, and on the transfer of technology, thereby closing the knowledge gap.

The success in East Asia is markedly different from the experience in many other countries of the world. The important point is that they did manage that process of globalization. For instance, China still has not opened its capital markets to short-term capital flows. They were able to demonstrate that you could get direct investment even when you do not open your markets to short-term capital flows. The rest of East Asia showed very strongly that opening the markets to short-term capital flow exposes you to enormous volatility without growth. It is risk without reward.

The problem is that, in much of the rest of the world, globalization has not been managed well. I believe that the advice and policies that have been pushed on many developing countries, sometimes called the Washington Consensus, has, in many cases, led to disastrous results. For instance, in Latin America, which at one time was rated as the best student of these policies, we have now a little more than a decade of data on how the region has performed under reform—and the central issue of reform is integration and globalization. However, the growth during the past decade is just over half of what it was in the fifties, sixties, and seventies, before reform. If this is success, then it is no wonder people are raising questions. Moreover, there were an enormous number of losers who have to live on $2 a day. The percentage of the population of Latin America, not only the absolute numbers, has increased. The percentage of the population that is unemployed has increased by about 3 percentage points. There is absolutely no doubt that globalization has not worked in the way that was promised. I would argue that many of the failures were directly related to the way globalization was managed in these countries. Globalization, as it was managed, exposed them to risk and volatility, and, in almost all cases, it is the poor that bear the consequences of that risk and volatility.

The underlying problem is that economic globalization has outpaced other dimensions of globalization, including political globalization, a sense of global social justice or a sense of global social solidarity. There is now an environment of unbalanced globalization. To put it another way, as the countries of the world get more closely integrated, you have more interdependence. But with more interdependence you need more collective action. You need to work together. You have more externalities. When you have collective action, you need to have mechanisms for making collective decisions. And we need to have those decisions be made in a multilateral way.

The problem is that our global institutional development has not kept pace with globalization. I want to illustrate what that implies by high-lighting four problems that I think have marked globalization in recent years. The first is that it has often been based on inequities, and those inequities have contributed to poverty. Take the global trade regime as just one example. There has been trade globalization, but it has been asymmetric. The United States and Western Europe have continued with huge subsidies to agriculture. World Bank studies show that, after the last round of trade negotiations, it was not just that the United States and Western Europe got the lion's share of the gains. You sort of expect that given their bargaining power, but in fact, some of their gains were at the expense of the poor countries. The studies also show that, because of terms of trade effects, the poorest regions of the world, especially in Africa, were actually worse off by about 2 percent.

The same thing is true of the intellectual property regime, which has threatened the ability of people in less-developed countries to get access to life-saving drugs. The United States and one or two other countries remain holdouts in reforming the intellectual property regime to address this problem, even though there has now been a resolve to address some of the problems of the past.

The second problem is that you would have expected, in a well-functioning global financial market, that the rich countries would bear the risk of interest rates and exchange-rate risks. In fact, when the poor countries borrow from the rich, the poor countries are forced to bear that risk. A result of this occurred during Latin American crisis of the early 1980s when, not through any fault of their own, the U.S. Federal Reserve raises interest rates to unheard-of levels, and the countries of Latin America were forced into bankruptcy.

The global reserve system is another example of a market failure. Poor countries around the world are forced, in effect, to hold reserves, which means that they are lending money to the U.S. government or Europe at very low interest rates, at the same time that they are borrowing at much higher rates of 15 to 20 percent in other contexts. That means, of course, that there is a net transfer. The inequity of this is obvious, but it also contributes to the global instability that we have seen in the early years of the new century.

The global financial institutions have not addressed the fundamental problems that will make globalization work better by enhancing stability.

The third problem is that the international economic institutions have pushed a particular variant of capitalism. There are many different forms of capitalism, for example, Swedish and Japanese. But the variant of capitalism that has been pushed is not even the American variant of capitalism. It differs markedly from what we have in the United States. It is something that we rejected. For instance, many countries have been pushed to privatize social security, even though the United States has rejected that notion repeatedly. It has pushed a central bank that focuses exclusively on inflation, even though the United States has a central bank that focuses on employment growth and inflation and has rejected repeatedly the notion that it would focus only on inflation.

The fourth problem is the way globalization has been pursued has undermined democracy. And it has undermined democracy in, for instance, the way conditionality has been imposed. It has undermined democracy in some of the national economic institutions, such as of the central banks. And it has undermined global democracy in the unilateral way much of the decision-making has taken place.

I do think that globalization does offer enormous opportunities for the poor countries, especially for reducing poverty. However, in the way that it has been managed in recent years, it has not lived up to that potential. Our challenge is to reshape it.

One of the reasons for the complexity of globalization and the difficulty of reading this debate is that the record is very disparate, and the issue is not simply a matter of how the system is governed. There are more complicated processes in motion that I think are important.

On the positive side, why are there strong advocates of globalization? There have actually been hundreds of millions of people who have escaped from poverty during this period. The two most populous countries of the world, China and India, have done spectacularly well by any historical standard. China perhaps offers the most successful economic development pattern in history in terms of pace, and certainly in terms of numbers of people who have been pulled from absolute poverty into quite remarkable improvement where it counts: in nutrition, in life expectancy, in quality of shelter and access to water and sanitation, and into income security. India also, during the last ten years, has made marked advances which are now becoming evident with a combined population of 2.3 billion people, about 40 percent of the world's population.

If you look to other places in Southeast Asia, Mexico, and Brazil, there has been undoubted progress on many fronts, despite the volatility. People say, "Look, globalization works." Not so simple and not so fast, because at the same time hundreds of millions of the very poorest people in the world have suffered not just a failure to keep up, but absolute decline. This has been the same period of pandemic disease; the largest pandemic in modern history, perhaps eventually in all time, the AIDS pandemic; a resurgence of malaria, of tuberculosis, a collapse of health care systems, dramatic collapses of life expectancy in dozens of countries in sub-Saharan Africa, worsening food productivity. That is the same planet we are living in. We need to be able to reconcile those two observations.

It is, I believe, a more complicated story to begin to understand this. I believe in general terms that management counts, and the management has not been up to par, but part of what needs to be managed is a proper diagnosis. The diagnosis reveals some interesting things. First, if you try to understand why countries are both gaining and losing, it is fairly systematic. First, all of the high-income countries have continued to achieve growth. Their role in the world economy is that they are the place where innovation is taking place, and globalization has been kind to the innovation process—just as Adam Smith said it would be a long time ago. Another group of countries, the countries in the developing world, have been able to get into the international production system through FDI, technology transfers, and strategic alliances; they have been able to move from primary commodity production to manufacturers in services. If you look at who is part of that global production system, a Brazil, or a Mexico, or a China, or an India, you find economic growth and improvements of living standards.

Two categories of countries have seen significant decline. One is the post-Soviet transition virtually everywhere, because it was a collapse of a heavy industry that extended eleven time zones. The other is the oil states, which have all seen a collapse in their single-commodity export.

Then we come to the fifth category, which is where the poorest of the poor live in the world. They are the producers of primary commodities. Almost without exception, the primary commodities producers have had a miserable run of it. If you are starting as a primary commodities producer and you do not find a way to become integrated in manufacturers and services, the probability just in terms of the historical record of the last twenty years is that you probably experienced almost no growth or absolute decline.

Then if you look at how these countries shake out, who has done what, it is actually also fairly systematic. The large countries, the coastal countries, the countries in major sea routes, the countries close to the major economies have tended to grow. It is the small and inland countries that add up to several hundred million people, whether in the Andean region, in Central Asia, in sub-Saharan African, where you see globalization not only does not reach, it has also provided no benefit and, in some ways, has actually provided loss. There is a structural underpinning to what we are seeing. With that structure, what we are also seeing is the terrible visage of Malthusian crisis, because these are places not reached by globalization—because globalization is not going to Burkina Faso, sadly. It is not reaching the Central African Republic. It is not reaching the highlands of the Andes. It is not reaching Central Asia. What is happening in many of the poorest places of the world is that the population growth continues to be very rapid, 3 percent or more per year. Soil nutrient depletion is massive. Deforestation and ecological degradation is massive. Disease is surging and not controlled, because these countries are too poor to run health-care systems.

We tend to see that those countries that are left out of the process are not only not holding their own, they are in outright, frank collapse right now. The world system does not address their problems adequately, because to address their problems would require financial resources of a much larger extent and targeting than we have been able to mobilize through all the pleas, and all the calls for help, and all the statements of support.

What does it mean to have inadequate financial reserves? It means death on a massive scale of people who have absolutely no reason to die except that they are too poor to stay alive.

In the WHO commission that I chaired in 2000 and 2001, we systematically—for the first and only time it has been done—calculated how much it would cost to keep people alive by extending essential life services, health services, whether for AIDS, TB, malaria, diarrheal disease, respiratory infection, immunization, or women that could have emergency obstetrical care so that half a million women would not die in childbirth every year, as they do now in the poorest countries. We found out that it would be $25 billion a year through a quite rigorous calculation led by the London School of Hygiene and Tropical Medicine. That is one thousandth of the rich world GNP. That is asking the rich world to put 10 cents of every $100 of income—10 cents into the efforts to fight killer disease in impoverished countries. If they did that, our epidemiologists calculated that this would avert 8 million deaths per year. We could be saving tens of millions of lives every year by understanding the structural collapse that is plaguing the poorest of the poor. Instead of sending lecturers from Washington, we ought to be sending medicines.

We ought to be addressing the real needs of ecological degradation, disease, the need for safe reproductive health services, children in school, and the other millennium development goals, which the secretary-general has been the most magnificent champion of, and help to bring in front of the world's eyes that these are things that can be achieved if we invest in them, if we recognize their urgency, and if we recognize that lectures and management will not be enough without real help.

It is the will, it is the attention to the needs of the poor, and it is the financial means all together to address those needs and to recognize that, by doing so, not only would we make a world that is vastly healthier and better educated, we will also make a world that is vastly more secure.

5

Who Is Afraid of Human Rights?

ALI MAZRUI AND WILLIAM F. SCHULZ

Ali Mazrui

The issue of whether human rights are universal is inevitably linked to the wider issue of whether there is such a thing as a universal moral standard or a universal ethical code. I argue that there is indeed a universal moral standard, but we do not know it yet. What will one day be acknowledged as universal is unfolding slowly. There are denominations of Islam that believe in a Hidden Imam guiding us mysteriously without being seen. I believe universal human rights are the equivalent of a Hidden Imam, revealing himself slowly but not yet completely.

Just as no one should be afraid of the Hidden Imam as a benevolent force in history, no one need be afraid of universal human rights either. We will gradually identify those rights, partly through the old utilitarian principle of minimization of pain and maximization of happiness in human experience.

Nineteenth-century Western political thinkers like Jeremy Bentham, James Mill, and John Stuart Mill developed a moral code based on the principle of the greatest happiness of the greatest number. This utilitarian philosophy had both strengths and weaknesses. But it needs to be reexamined in the light of the ultimate code of human rights, revealing itself slowly out of the womb of human history. Human rights and human obligations need to be balanced in such a way that the sum of human happiness is optimized and the sum of human pain is minimized.

The Hidden Imam of human rights reveals itself in installments. Shakespeare once proposed that there was nothing either right or wrong, good or bad, but thinking made it so. But what people thought in Shakespeare's time is very different from what they think today. Changing perceptions across time inevitably result in changing standards across generations. If moral judgments vary across time from decade to decade, why should they not differ across cultures?

Moral variations across time may be called historical relativism (cross-cultural). Moral variations across societies may be called cultural relativism (cross-societal). What was okay in the past and is not okay now is historical relativism. What is okay in Kuala Lumpur but is not okay in New York City is cultural relativism.

These variations affect leadership and its ethics across time and across cultures. Regarding the Clinton-Lewinsky scandal: was it adultery or lying under oath that was worse? In Islam it was the adultery that was the bigger threat to the social order of the family.

Homosexuality in the first half of the twentieth century was a crime almost everywhere in the world. Since the second half of the twentieth century, it has been legalized in most of the Western world. But are we ready yet for a gay president of the United States?

The death penalty has been abolished in Canada, western Europe, and at least thirty other countries. It may one day be regarded as a violation of human rights in the United States. But we are not yet ready for a U.S. president who is against the death penalty.

There used to be a time when some religions regarded the souls of women as less important than the souls of men. Now much of that has changed, because there has been an important revolution in the interpretation of the rights of women, both in this world and in spiritual terms.

The definition of corruption in the United States has tightened in the last forty years. John F. Kennedy, as president, nominated his own brother, Robert Kennedy, to be attorney general. By the standards of

1961, that was acceptable. By the standards of today, it would be regarded as nepotistic and corrupt.

I personally believe there is a universal moral standard that cuts across cultures and across epochs, but we do not as yet know what it is. The universal moral standard is being revealed slowly by human history—but human history may still have a way to go.

It is like the doctrine of predestination in Islam or Calvinism. We may believe everything is preordained, but we have no idea where the destination is.

In Calvinism, the answer is to look for signs of the destination, signals of salvation. They are not conclusive, but they may be road signs: "Inna Shaqqiya la Shaqqiyul azali," "Wa 'aksuhu' saidu Iam yubaddali."

Similarly, with universal moral standards, we just look for signs as to what is universal. For example, incest is almost universally regarded as sinful. Matricide (mother killing child or vice versa) may be regarded as a universal sense of revulsion. A ban on torturing and killing babies may be universal. Are we revolted when they are tortured because the babies are innocent or because they are young? If we are revolted by baby-torturing because babies are innocent, then we may decide that torturing any innocent person by extension is wrong. If there is torture in Baghdad and Guantanamo Bay today, it may be wrong even if the purpose is right.

Most of us have reached that conclusion. But these are signs that there is probably a universal standard. These signs do not themselves constitute *the* universal standard.

Finally, a word about the distinction between human rights and civil rights. Civil rights and civil liberties are specific to particular countries. Human rights are supposed to be valid for the whole of the human species.

The right to marry across racial differences, interracial marriage, is a human right. The right to marry a person of your own sex, gay marriage, is a civil right in the state of Massachusetts. Interracial marriage has evolved into a universal human right. Same-sex marriages, on the other hand, are unlikely to be included in a future United Nations Declaration of Human Rights. At best, gay rights are civil rights in more and more societies but seem unlikely to be accepted as universal human rights in all societies.

And, yet, who knows? If the truly universal ethical code is in the womb of history, and is only revealing itself slowly in installments, even gay rights may one day be raised from the status of civil rights in Western societies to the status of human rights across the world. After all, the Hidden Imam of Secular Ethics has yet to pronounce his final fatwa of governance.

William Schulz

I heard some time ago that the three most popular topics for books in the United States are sex, dogs, and Abraham Lincoln. Ever since then I have wanted to write a book about the sex lives of Abraham Lincoln's dogs but the data on that topic is scarce and so I have been reduced to writing books about human rights. I am very grateful to the secretary-general for the opportunity to be a part of this panel.

The title of this panel is a provocative one: "Who's Afraid of Human Rights?" I am tempted to answer either "no one" or "everyone."

If "no one" is the proper answer, it is simply because human rights remain more of a dream than a reality for much of the world. Lacking, as we do, effective, consistent structures of accountability for enforcing human rights—things like a standing international army that can be called upon in the face of significant abuse—human rights remain little more than a nice idea for millions of the earth's people, Darfur, in Sudan, being one of the best examples of that today.

Moreover, those who are responsible for some of the worst human rights violations, namely, nonstate actors who may fairly be accused of employing terrorist tactics, are even less susceptible to the human rights vision than many governments. One is hard-pressed to imagine an Osama bin Laden, for example, perusing a UN resolution calling on him to cease and desist from violence or opening thousands of letters from Amnesty activists and suddenly seeing the error of his ways and proclaiming, "By jove, I think they're right!" The world has not even been able to agree on a common definition of terrorism, much less an international treaty against it, and hence governments are free to call anyone they like, including their peaceful democratic opponents, terrorists with little fear of international opprobrium.

So one answer to the topic question may well be "no one" but, if that is the answer, then why, we might ask, do so many governments, military officials, corporations, and political pundits spend so much time and energy pretending that they are champions of human rights and debunking any criticisms that might tarnish such an image? When we human rights advocates issue critical reports on governments, we often feel like the actor to whom Sam Goldwyn, the famous movie producer, once said, "When I want your opinion, I'll give it to you."

Who, then, is afraid of human rights and why? The list of the timorous is a long one.

Small countries are afraid of human rights because they may be utilized as an excuse to compromise their sovereignty. Human rights have become in good measure the plumb line against which to gauge degrees of international respectability and a government that is blatant in its violations risks becoming a pariah state, if not a "liberated" one.

Large countries are afraid of human rights because they provide limits to their autonomy. Human rights and humanitarian law, after all, define the boundaries beyond which those who pride themselves on civilized behavior may not go.

Some years ago, I and my colleagues in the U.S. human rights movement met with top officials at the Bush administration's National Security Council and the Pentagon to beg them to take seriously reports we had received of mistreatment of prisoners in U.S. custody. It now appears that our pleas were ignored not because those officials took them too casually but because they took them all too seriously, but believed the mistreatment was justified in a world in which, after 9/11, all the rules were repeatedly said to have changed. Those officials no doubt knew that exposure of the crimes—what we were calling for—would do enormous damage, as it has, to the U.S. claim to be acting in defense of civilized values and the rule of law.

The Bush administration was afraid of human rights—be it in its violations of the Geneva Convention with respect to the status of prisoners at Guantanamo or in its denial of the right to legal counsel of Jose Padilla and Yaser Hamdi or any number of other instances—because adherence to international structures is enormously inconvenient. It requires, for one thing, recognition of the viability of the concept of an international community but, as Condoleezza Rice wrote in *Foreign Affairs* magazine during the 2000 presidential campaign, "Foreign policy in a Republican administration . . . will proceed from the firm ground of the national interest, not from the interests of an illusory international community." Human rights are one of the most visible manifestations of that most inconvenient illusion.

But governments, small or large, are far from the only ones who fear human rights. Some military officials find them a pain because they rest on the presupposition that all blood flows red and that our adversaries are human too. One of the great myths of our age is that it is psychologically easy to induce one human being to kill another. If that were true, armies would not spend so much time providing their soldiers with rationales for doing what supposedly came naturally. But the dehumanization of our adversaries—the transforming of *adversary* into *enemy*—is a key component of most training for war. Human rights advocates are not all pacifists by any means, but they do insist that no one sacrifices their fundamental humanness merely by taking up arms.

And then consider the business community. International corporations are generally among those most fearful, if not derisive, of human rights because violations can cost them money in the form of sullied reputation, disenchanted customers, expensive monitoring and retraining of contractors, and lost revenue from governments and international financial institutions. Many companies have gradually come to recognize that respect for human rights is actually good for business, but it is hard to avoid the perception that, all things being equal, many corporate titans would just as soon have we human rights workers crawl back into the holes from which we have come.

And no doubt that is sometimes true of the United Nations itself, which is another institution that may on occasion be afraid of human rights because human rights standards magnify its failures. After all, protection of human rights is not always compatible with maintenance of peace and, though we know that in the long run peace and justice go hand in hand, in the short run the pursuit of justice may be anything but tranquil.

Which leads to a final group of people who are afraid of human rights, and that is the human rights community itself. In the first place, we in the Western human rights community have been sorely and appropriately challenged in the last few years to expand our understanding of human rights to include social and economic rights, not just the traditional civil and political rights, and to make way for the wisdom and leadership of emerging indigenous human rights champions. And, in the second place, to be a true advocate of human rights is to be an equal opportunity critic and hence the least popular guy or gal at the dance. It is to disavow both Cuba's imprisonment of political dissidents *and* the U.S. embargo of Cuba. It is to condemn Palestinian suicide bombers *and* the human rights violations of the Israeli Defense Forces. It is to chastise governments for abusing human rights in the name of fighting terrorism *and* disdain all killing of civilians in a larger political or religious cause. And hence it is to bring everybody's wrath upon one's head, which is, I suppose, how we know we are doing our job.

And when we do that job inadequately, we deserve to be censured ourselves. In an essay in the *New York Times Magazine*, for instance, I reminded the human rights community, focused as we have been on opposing violations of liberty in the name of security, that, under Article 3 of the Universal Declaration of Human Rights, being safe in one's home is every bit as much a human rights as having a fair trial, and I reminded readers that Stephen Spender, a firm supporter of the opponents of Franco in the Spanish Civil War, gradually came to question one aspect of his own conduct. "When I saw photographs of children murdered by [Franco's] Fascists," he wrote in *The God That Failed*, "I felt furious pity. [But] when the supporters of Franco talked of [our own] atrocities, I merely felt indignant that people could tell such lies. In the first case I saw corpses, in the second only words. . . . I gradually acquired a certain horror at the way my own mind worked. . . . It was clear to me that unless I cared about every murdered child impartially, I did not care about children being murdered at all."

So these are some of those who are afraid of human rights—though of course in every category there are exceptions to the rule—and this is also why international civil society is so important to the creation and maintenance of the human rights regimen. Because each of the institutions I have mentioned, including human rights NGOs, has its own narrow interests and only a truly global civil society has any chance at all of surmounting that parochialism.

Then, too, while the world will never agree on what constitutes a religious basis for human rights—those who drafted the Universal Declaration tried to agree on its religious roots and almost came to blows over the exercise—and while we will never agree on those qualities of the human creature that are sufficient to ground human rights in natural law—Isak Dinessen once said, "What is a human being, after all, but an elaborate machine for turning red wine into urine?"—it is far harder to dispute the notion that pouring hot oil over one's enemies' heads or selling human beings as chattel or raping women at a man's pleasure are any longer respectable forms of human behavior. The reason they are not is because the concept of an international community is not an illusion, and it is that very community, through its treaties and legal mechanisms and political and economic institutions, through which those human rights norms evolve and change and thrive.

The final reason international civil society is so important to the human rights enterprise is because it embodies the human capacity for moral imagination without which the human community itself would perish.

With all of the justifiable criticism that was leveled at those military police at Abu Ghraib prison and at their military superiors and at their civilian Pentagon bosses, I would like to reserve just a modicum of outrage for all those experts and pundits and academics who assured us in the months following 9/11 that torture was now an acceptable option—people like Jonathan Alter in *Newsweek* and Bruce Hoffman in *The Atlantic* and Alan Dershowitz everywhere there was a camera. What each of them suffered from was not stupidity—they are very bright people—or even hubris but a paucity of moral imagination.

In the midst of the 1994 Rwandan genocide, according to Philip Gourrevitch, a girl's school was attacked by machete-wielding militiamen in the middle of the night. The teenagers were rousted from their beds about two o'clock in the morning and forced to line up in the dining hall. They were ordered to separate themselves, Hutu from Tutsi, so that only the Tutsi would die. But the girls refused. A second time the commander ordered them to divide themselves up by ethnic group. But still they refused. And finally—this is what it was reported later—one of the girls found her voice and, though very frightened, said, "We cannot separate ourselves, you see, because we are not Hutu. We are not Tutsi. We are Rwandan," at which point every one of them was slaughtered.

But what a legacy they leave! "We are not Hutu. We are not Tutsi. We are Rwandan." That sentiment bespeaks a graciousness for which the world is desperate. In her magnificent essay "The Moral Necessity of Metaphor," the novelist Cynthia Ozick quotes this passage from the Hebrew Scriptures, Leviticus, chapter 19: "The stranger that sojourned with you shall be unto you as the home-born among you and you shall love him as yourself for you too were strangers in the land of Egypt." She goes on to say that it is exactly because we too were once strangers in the land of Egypt that we can identify with another, that "doctors can imagine what it is to be patients. Those who have no pain can imagine what it is to suffer. Those at the center can imagine what it is to be outside. The strong can imagine what it is to be weak. . . . And we strangers can imagine the familiar hearts of [other] strangers."

Human rights emerge out of the common misery of humankind and give voice to the simplest needs of the human spirit—needs for things like the reconciliation of adversaries and a fair distribution of the earth's abundance. They teach us that evil is real but that evil will perish if we but cleave to the moral imagination. Who is afraid of human rights? Almost all of us. But with the help of that imagination may emerge a new sense of outrage, a new vision of justice and a new form of courage. Thank you for all that you do in this place to see that that one day may be true.

Identity and Religion

Identity in the Twenty-First Century

AMARTYA SEN AND KWAME ANTHONY APPIAH

Amartya Sen

It is a tremendous privilege to speak here today at this meeting arranged by, and chaired by, Kofi Annan, the outstanding secretary-general of our United Nations, for whom I have boundless admiration, and to speak jointly with Anthony Appiah, a visionary thinker and friend whose ideas have influenced me greatly.

We live in a divided world, partitioned by economic inequality and political disaffection, but also increasingly by the bellicose cultivation of some single categorization of human beings, deeply reducing the richness of being human. The use of a uniquely divisive identity manifests itself in many forms in distinct areas of social interaction. People have been made to fight each other to assert the imagined demands of their allegedly singular identity, respectively along the lines of race, religion, ethnicity, or nationality, expressing itself in race riots, communal slaughter, or political butchery—in each case drowning all the other affiliations of the persons different from the particular singularity being championed in that ideologically engineered battle.

At the global level, the divisiveness of unique categorization increasingly takes the form of championing a hard and allegedly impenetrable division along the lines of religion, or religion-based understanding of civilization. The twentieth century came to its end with a rash of theories—explicitly formulated or implicitly advanced—on the so-called clash of civilizations. Indeed, very often now, the politics of global confrontation is taken to be a corollary of religious or cultural divisions in the world, and the world is increasingly seen, if only indirectly, as a collectivity of religions, or of so-called civilizations defined primarily according to religion, thereby ignoring all the other hundreds of ways in which people see themselves. Underlying all this is the odd assumption that the people of the world can be uniquely categorized according to some singular and overarching system of partitioning.

The newly popular singular view of identity is not only incendiary and dangerous, it is also astonishingly naive. In our normal lives, we see ourselves as members of a variety of groups—we belong to all of them. The same person can be, without any contradiction, a U.S. citizen, of Asian background, of Indochinese origin, with Vietnamese ancestry, a Christian, a liberal, a woman, a vegetarian, a historian, a school teacher, a novelist, a feminist, a heterosexual, a believer in gay and lesbian rights, a theater lover, an environmental activist, a tennis fan, a sprinter, a committed jazz musician. A person has many affiliations, some quite standard (in many ways entirely ordinarily, such as being rich or poor, or a woman or a man), others rather special, even eccentric (sometimes very eccentric). But each of these collectivities, to all of which this person simultaneously belongs, gives her a particular identity, which can be, depending on the context and circumstances, extremely important for her behavior and priorities.

Given our inescapably plural identities, we have to decide on—choose between—the relative importance of our different associations and affiliations in any particular context. If the terrorist and other instigators of violence try to cultivate and exploit the illusion of singularity, that work is made more easy for them by the singular partition of the world population according to some overarching criterion of civilizational identity. Whether civilizational categorizers go on from there to champion a thesis of clash of civilization (which is now a much travelled route), or take to the cosy and warm road of recommending dialogue among civilizations (which is a far nicer sentiment and not entirely unpopular at the United Nations itself), there is a shared misconception in both the approaches that the relations between different human beings, with all their diversities, can be somehow captured in the form of relations between civilizations, rather than between persons. Both approaches undermine, in one way or another, our need to think about our variety of affiliations and associations, and the need to take responsibility for our choices.

One example of the harm this does is well illustrated by the way the world heritage of science and mathematics has been appropriated by the Western world through seeing modern science and mathematics as quintessentially Western (even though the origin of many of the basic mathematical or scientific concepts came from elsewhere). For example, when an American mathematician today invokes an algorithm to solve a difficult computational problem, she helps to commemorate—typically without knowing it—the contributions of the ninth-century Muslim mathematician, Al-Khwarizmi, from whose name the term *algorithm* is derived (the term *algebra* comes from his Arabic book, *Al Jabr wa-al-Muqabilah*). Despite the importance of this Arab heritage and Muslim history, crude civilizational classifications have tended to put science and mathematics in the basket of Western science, leaving other civilizations to mine their pride in religious depths. The non-Western activists, then, focus on those issues that divide them from the West (such as particular religious beliefs, distinctive local customs, and cultural specificities), rather than on those things that reflect global interactions (including science, mathematics, literature, music, storytelling, and so on). The congruence between Western parochialists and Islamic extremists (neither sees much of interest in Al-Khwarizmi, for example) is one of the more pernicious implicit alliances at the beginning of our new century.

Something similar can be said about the way Western parochialism has captured the fundamental idea of decisions through public discussion, which can be seen as the basis of deliberative democracy in the modern world. The long tradition of such deliberations in Africa, in India, in Iran and West Asia, in China, Japan, and East Asia is comprehensively ignored to create a peculiar thesis of Western exceptionalism. The defenders of this bit of shallow history often use every possible deflection to distract attention from the widespread history of toleration and dialogue in the world, along with the history of intolerance that can be also be found across the globe. The thesis of the exclusively Western origin of deliberative democracy can be sustained by an odd combination of ignoring the examples of tolerance in non-Western cultures as well as cases of manifest intolerance within the Western heritage.

No significance is attached, for example, to the fact that when the heretic Giordano Bruno was burnt at the stake in Rome for his apostasy, the Indian emperor Akbar, himself a Muslim, had just concluded his project of codifying the rights of every citizen to have freedom of religion, and had just completed several intense rounds of discussion involving the different religious communities, Hindus, Muslims, Christians, Jews, Parsees, Jains, and others, including atheists. The occurrence of persecution under European inquisitions, or for that matter under Nazi rule, is taken implicitly to be insignificant, whereas cases of intolerance in Muslim history and in the history of other non-Western societies are regarded as powerful evidence of omnipresent evidence of intolerance in those societies and this serves as the alleged empirical basis for developing a monolithic theory of the uniquely and quintessentially—and uniquely—"Western" character of tolerance and social deliberation.

The lessons drawn from this distorted history cannot, of course, escape being based on elaborate and motivated selection. And it is this oddly biased selection that is taken to provide evidential support to the strangely formulaic story of Western liberalism contrasted with intolerance in the rest of the world that deserves much more scrutiny than it tends to get.

The crudity of civilizational thinking generated by singularist illusion not only debilitates our understanding of world history and of the contemporary world, and hampers an adequately broad understanding of the causal influences behind the recent developments of global terrorism, it also obstructs clarity of thought on a variety of policy issues. The ways and means of resisting global terrorism are among the subjects that are not well served by the reductionist rhetoric. There are, however, many other policy issues on which the narrowness of civilizational thinking also imposes an artificial barrier, including the assessment of problems of immigration from one country to another.

No matter how serious the practical problems of having relatively easy immigration from other countries may be (and it is not hard to think of difficult problems that are real, not imaginary), we must also take note of the fact that historically civilizations have greatly benefited from the immigration of people as well as of ideas. Indeed, ideas have often rapidly spread with movements of people. I am not suggesting that a broad understanding of the fruitfulness of across-border movements should dominate and outweigh all the arguments that may be presented against such movements, but we are not likely to get an adequately objective resolution of specific problems if we are determined to keep general considerations out of the accounting altogether. The specificity of a problem includes a description of its size and domain. The invitation to be both narrow and narrow-minded can certainly be resisted through looking at real—rather than imagined—history. The history of Europe, Asia, Africa, and America would be very incomplete if the cross-border migrations were taken to be of no consequence. Because the view of clash of civilizations tends to promote, if only implicitly, a highly limited understanding of civilizational history, it is particularly important that the broad and the general issues are also brought out into the open.

If the folly of civilizational thinking is a prime example of the harm that solitarist categorization does, there are many other applications of basically the same denuded approach in other arenas of social interaction. Indeed, even the problem of immigration itself involves many other excessive simplifications related to the temptation to attribute unique importance to some particular human identity. To illustrate the reach and wide range of the problem, let me turn briefly to some of the issues that may not be getting their due in the country in which we are right now, viz, the United States, in its debates on illegal immigration and the identity of language and literature.

Consider, for example, the hyped-up demand for expelling all illegal immigrants from the United States, which has gained some ground recently, despite this country's wonderful history of welcoming new entrants. As I give this talk, a battle is still to come on this subject in the House of Representatives, even though the Senate has taken a less rigidly punitive view.

Illegal immigrants do, of course, have the identity of being immigrants as well as illegal in status, and this must be significant for public policy. However, with suitable propaganda, many already settled Americans—particularly those nervous about their jobs—may be persuaded to see the identity of an illegal immigrant as being just "illegal" (as if it were a total description of these people). And yet they have other identities too, not just in terms of their shared humanity and their shared concerns about their children, families, and neighborhoods, but also in terms of the work they do, the particular role they play in the economy, and the global perspectives they bring—directly or indirectly—to American public reasoning.

In an essay titled "Enforceable, Sustainable, Compassionate," Michael Bloomberg, the mayor of New York, has argued that not only is "the idea of deporting 11 million people, nearly as many as live in the entire state of Illinois," one of "pure fantasy," but also "if it were attempted, it would devastate both families and our economy." We have to look for other solutions that do justice to the multidimensionality of human beings. Bloomberg has gone on to suggest a mixed policy of, on the one hand, reducing the incentive to immigrate and the ease of doing so, and, on the other hand, expanding lawful opportunities that immigrants in general have. The basic conceptual issue here lies in the recognition that while an illegal immigrant is indeed "that," he or she is not "just that," so that an enlightened public policy has to see the other identities and other roles of these very same people, even as legality is pursued.

There is also an important issue of identity in the treatment of those who have already immigrated, and are settled here—in the United States—now, whether or not they have already become American citizens. In that context, the question of language is an important one. Should everyone be required to learn English? Certainly, there is a clear case for everyone who settles in this country to be able to manage English, and what we can fruitfully discuss are the ways and means to bring this about.

What is particularly pernicious, however, is the proposal that has received considerable airing, that there should be no entitlement to have the federal laws and other legal facilities explained to people in any language other than English. This can make sense only through another profound confusion between the kind of linguistic identity a person should ideally have (in particular, being able to speak English, in addition to whatever other language the person might have been reared in) and what linguistic identity a person actually does have, which may fall far short of the ideal, at any given time, if a person does not actually follow English adequately, possibly despite best efforts. Access to the laws and rules about facilities is a part of the basic rights of people, and the significant identity of human beings as persons with these rights cannot be arbitrarily removed on the punitive ground of linguistic shortcoming.

There is also a very general consideration that may be brought in to supplement the particular concerns on which I have been concentrating in the last few minutes. A lot of the violence in the world is now being cultivated by a singular focus on the religious identity of human beings, as if nothing else matters. In that context, to argue for the importance of another classificatory device—different from religion—namely, the languages you speak and are comfortable with is, I believe, a contribution toward defusing the cultivated brutality of interreligious strifes.

This argument does not run counter to the importance of learning English if a person is going to live in this country, but it does go against the folly of assuming that making everybody unilingual—everyone speaking only English—would be a desirable move. Not only does the diversity of language and literature enrich human lives, but also the recognition of the importance of languages can compete with the univocal and sometimes devastatingly singular concentration on religious divisions only.

Language has played that role in many political movements. For example, the separation of Bangladesh with a focus on the Bengali language had the effect of making it easier for Bangladesh to develop nonreligious—indeed secular—politics, and also helped the sizeable non-Muslim population of Bangladesh become more integrated with the mainstream, because they do share the Bengali language, regardless of religion. Indeed, in the burying of the remnant memory of Hindu-Muslim riots from the 1940s, which had occurred in what is now Bangladesh as well (like in the rest of the subcontinent), the alternative focus on language has had a powerfully soothing effect, a constructive process that began fairly soon after the partition of the subcontinent in 1947 (well before the ultimate birth of Bangladesh in 1971).

The general point about identity here is that by focusing on another basis of identification—other than religion—something is gained in today's world by reducing the univocal severity of religious conflicts. The tendency in the contemporary world to privilege exactly one identity over all others has done a great deal of harm already, in fomenting racial violence, communal strife, religion-related terrorism, suppression of immigrants, denial of basic human rights, and so on. There is a parallel in the role that national divisions—and citizenships—played in the first half of the twentieth century, in the first world war, when the British, the French, and the Germans decimated each other along nationally patriotic lines. Unique prioritization of national identities played a pernicious role then in a way that has many parallels to the use of religious divisions today as a uniquely important divisive line in the cultivated fomenting of contemporary discord and allegedly civilizational clash.

As the new century takes its course, it is important to reassert the fullness of human beings—not miniaturized by a singular identity. We have to resist being put into little boxes in which the artisans of disaffection and terror want to confine us. The glory of being human cannot be captured by any one narrow categorization. That, I would argue, is the central challenge of identity-based thinking at the beginning of the twenty-first century.

Kwame Anthony Appiah

I am very grateful to the secretary-general for doing me the honor of inviting me to speak here at the United Nations, and more specifically for the honor that I feel doing so in the company of Amartya Sen, one of the towering intellectual figures of the world today.

I would like to talk briefly today about cosmopolitanism—a philosophical ideal that I think can be especially useful in facing those conflicts grounded in religious, ethnic, racial, and national identities that pervade our world, challenging so often the international institutions whose symbolic heart is in this building.

As it happens, it is an ideal whose name comes to us from the classical West. Its etymology is Greek—even though the man who coined the term came, like so many Western traditions, from Asia Minor—because the earliest person we know of who said that he was a citizen of the world, a *kosmou polites* in Greek, which is where of course our word *cosmopolitan* comes from, was Diogenes, philosopher and founder of the philosophical movement called Cynicism.

Diogenes was born sometime late in the fifth century in Sinope on the southern coast of the Black Sea in what is now Turkey. The Cynics rejected tradition and local loyalty and generally opposed what every-one else thought of as civilized behavior. Diogenes himself lived naked in a large terra cotta pot. It is said, too, that he did what my English nanny would have called "his business" in public. Worse yet, he did what Hugh Hefner has made his business in public as well. So he was sort of a fourth century BCE version of what a contemporary New Yorker would call a performance artist. And he was called a Cynic—*kynikos* in Greek means dog-like—because he lived like a dog. It is no wonder that they kicked him out of Sinope.

But, as I say, for better or worse, Diogenes is the first person who is reported to have said that he was a citizen of the world. This is a meta-phor, of course, because citizens share a state, and there was no world state—no Cosmopolis—for Diogenes to be a citizen of. So, like anyone who adopts this metaphor, he had to decide what to mean by it.

One thing that Diogenes didn't mean was that he favored unitary world government. He once met someone who did, Alexander the Great, who favored, as you know, government of the world by Alexander the Great. The story goes that Alexander came across Diogenes one sunny day, this time for some reason not in his usual pot but in a hole in the ground. The Macedonian world conqueror, who was Aristotle's student and had been brought up to respect philosophers, asked Diogenes if there was anything he could do for him. "Sure," Diogenes said, or what-ever the equivalent in ancient Greek is of *sure*. "You can get out of my light." So Diogenes was clearly not a fan of Alexander's or, as we may suppose, of Alexander's project of global domination. (This, by the way, must have upset Alexander, who was supposed to have said once, "If I had not been Alexander, I should have liked to have been Diogenes.")

So the first thing I would like to take from Diogenes in interpreting the metaphor of global citizenship is: no world government, not even by a student of Aristotle's. We can think of ourselves, Diogenes wanted to say, as fellow citizens, even if we are not and do not want to be mem-bers of a single political community, subject to a single government.

The second idea we can take from Diogenes is we should care about the fate of all our fellow human beings, not just those in our own politi-cal community. Just as within your community you must care about your own fellow citizens, so in the global world community as a whole, you should care for your fellow world citizens, your fellow humans. And furthermore—this is the third idea of Diogenes—we can borrow good ideas from all over the world, not just from within our own society. It is worth listening to others because they may have something to teach us. It is worth their listening to us because they may have something to learn. That is a final thing I want to borrow from Diogenes—the value of dialogue—conversation as a fundamental mode of human communication.

These three ideas, then, I, a twenty-first-century American citizen of Anglo-Ghanaian ancestry, want to borrow from a citizen of Sinope who dreamed of global citizenship twenty-four centuries ago:

- One, we don't need a single world government.
- Two, we must care for the fate of all human beings inside and outside our own societies.
- Three, we have much to gain from conversations with one another across differences.

Diogenes's cosmopolitanism entered western intellectual history through the Stoics; and cosmopolitanism, as Diogenes understood it, with its openness to foreigners without embracing world government, is found in the greatest of the Stoics—in Cicero, for example, and in the emperor Marcus Aurelius. If anyone should have believed in world government, it was these Roman rulers of the world; but Marcus Aurelius talked about cosmopolitanism to insist on the spiritual affinity of all human beings, not to argue for a global empire.

Through people like Cicero and Aurelius, Stoicism entered the intellectual life of Christendom.

You can hear these Stoic echoes in the language of a Greek-speaking Jew named Saul from Tarsus, another town in Asia Minor. Saul was a Hellenized Roman citizen, known to history of course as St. Paul, the great institutional architect of the Christian church. In his epistle to the Galatians, he wrote famously, "There is neither Jew nor Greek. There is neither bond nor free. There is neither male nor female, for ye are all one in Christ Jesus."

One of my favorite facts is that Sinope, Diogenes's hometown, was in Galatia. So St. Paul, when he wrote those very cosmopolitan words, was writing to Diogenes's people, to the very people who gave the world the first cosmopolitan.

When the idea of cosmopolitanism was taken up again in the European enlightenment, it had the same call: global concern for humanity without a wish for a single world government. Modern cosmopolitanism grew with nationalism, not as an alternative but as a complement to it, and at its heart, with not just the idea of universality, concern for all humanity as fellow citizens, but also the value of different human ways of going on.

That is why it does not go with world government—because different communities are entitled to live according to different standards because human beings can flourish in different forms of society because so many values are worth living by, and nobody—and no single society can explore them all.

You find cosmopolitanism in Herder, the great philosopher of German romanticism and German nationalism. Herder believed that the German-speaking peoples were entitled to live together in a single political community, but he also saw that what was good for the Germans was good for everyone else, and so unlike many Germans of his days he believed in the political self-determination of all the peoples of Europe—indeed of the world.

You find cosmopolitanism, too, in Immanuel Kant's plan for a perpetual peace, which was of course the origin of the idea of a league of nations, the forerunner therefore of the United Nations.

Cosmopolitanism, then, is universalistic. It believes that every human being matters and that we have a shared human obligation to care for one another, but it also accepts a wide range of legitimate human diversity, and that respect for diversity comes from something that also goes back to Diogenes: tolerance for other people's choices of how to live and humility about what we ourselves know.

Conversation across identities, across religions, races, ethnicities, and nationalities is worthwhile because through conversation you can learn from people with ideas different, even incompatible, from your own; and it is worthwhile, too, because if you accept that you live in a world with many kinds of people and you're going to try to live in a respectful peace with them, then you need to understand each other, even if you don't agree.

Globalization has made this ancient ideal relevant, which it really was not in Diogenes's or Aurelius's day. You see, there are two obvious conditions on making citizenship real: knowledge about the lives of other citizens and the power to affect them. And Diogenes did not know about most people—in China or Japan and the Americas and equatorial Africa or even western or northern Europe—and nothing he did was likely to have much impact on those other people, either. You cannot give real meaning to the idea that we are all fellow citizens if you cannot affect each other and you do not know about each other.

But as I say, we do not live in Diogenes's world. Only in the last few centuries, as every human community is gradually being drawn into a single web of trade and the global network of information, have we come to a point where each of us can realistically imagine sending any other of our six billion fellow human beings something worth having: a radio, an antibiotic, a good idea. Unfortunately, we can now also send, through negligence, as well as malice, things that cause harm: a virus, an airborne pollutant, a bad idea. And the possibilities of good and ill are multiplied beyond all measure when it comes to policies carried out by governments in our name.

Together, we can ruin poor farmers by dumping our subsidized drain into their markets, cripple industries by punitive tariffs, deliver weapons that will kill thousands upon thousands. That's the bad news. The good news is that, together, we can raise standards of living by adopting new policies on trade and aid, prevent or treat diseases with vaccines and pharmaceuticals, take measures against global climate change, encourage resistance to tyranny and a concern for the worth of each human life.

And of course the worldwide web of information—radio, television, telephones, the Internet—means not only that we can affect lives everywhere but also that we can learn about life everywhere, too. In short, the existence of global media means that we can now know about one another, and global interconnections—economic, political, military, ecological—mean that we will now affect one another. So now we really need a cosmopolitan spirit. That spirit thinks of us as bound to cross the species, bound together, but also accepts that we will make different choices within and across nations about how to make our lives.

Cosmopolitanism values cultural diversity because of what it makes possible for people. At the heart of modern cosmopolitanism is respect for the diversity of cultures not because cultures matter in themselves but because people matter, and culture matters to people.

So where culture is bad for people—individual men, women, and children—the cosmopolitan does not need to be tolerant of it. We do not need to treat genocide or human rights abuse as just another part of the quaint diversity of the species, a local taste that some totalitarians just happen to have.

Cosmopolitanism, then, is a double-standard tradition. In a slogan, it is universality plus difference.

I have already hinted at why cosmopolitans celebrate—more than accept but celebrate the wide range of legitimate human diversity. But I want to be more explicit about this. Why, after all, should we not do, in the name of universal concern, what missionaries of many faiths have done in the past? Why should we not go out into the world, guided by the truth, and help others to live by it, too?

One reason is that cosmopolitans inherit from our Greek forebears a recognition of the fallibility of human claims to knowledge. Cosmopolitanism begins, I think, with the philosophical doctrine of fallibilism, the recognition that we may be mistaken, even when we have looked carefully at the evidence and applied our highest mental capacities. A fallabilist knows that he or she is likely to make mistakes about things. We have views, and we take our own views seriously, but we are always open to the possibility that it may turn out that we were wrong. If I am wrong about something, maybe I can learn from others, even if they are wrong about something else.

But there is a second reason, one whose roots are in a more modern idea—the idea that each individual is charged with ultimate responsibility for her or his own life. The dignity of each human being resides in part exactly in the capacity for and right to self-management. Because of this, it is important that human beings live by standards they believe in, even if those standards are wrong. If I force a man to do what I take to be right, when he does not think it is right, or stop a woman from doing what I take to be wrong when she does not agree that it is wrong, I am often not making their lives better, even if what I take to be right or wrong really is right or wrong.

Of course, if the wrong someone is doing harms others, I may have to stop her anyway because the universal concern that underlies cosmopolitanism means that it matters to me that every human life should go well. But if she is of sound mind and the wrong she is planning to do affects only her fate, then the right way to express my concern for her is not to force her to do the right thing but to try to persuade her that she is mistaken.

Still, because cosmopolitanism is fallibilistic, cosmopolitan conversations across cultural and political and social and economic and religious boundaries will not be about wholesale conversion. These conversations will involve learning, as well as teaching, listening as well as talking. Even when I am trying to persuade someone that what they see as right is wrong, I am also hearing arguments that what I think is wrong is right.

Now, global conversation is a metaphor. It needs interpretation, just as the metaphor of global citizenship needs interpretation because of course you and I cannot literally converse with the other nearly seven billion strangers who inhabit the planet. But a global community of cosmopolitans will consist of people who want to learn about other ways of life, through travel and tourism, by reading anthropology, history, and novels, watching movies, and following the news in newspapers, on radio, on television, and on the Internet. Indeed, let me make my only entirely concrete, practical proposal, practical here in New York, at least. Cosmopolitans here should do what people all around the world are already doing with American movies—see at least one movie with subtitles a month.

7

God's Word and World Politics

DESMOND TUTU

It is a very great privilege to have been asked to share in the series of lectures sponsored by the secretary-general.

Well, you know when you have someone say, "Oh, he's very well known, and he does not need to be introduced." My wife and I were on a train in Atlanta, and somebody thought, "Ah." They recognized me, and they came and they asked for autographs, and I was signing autographs, and I was trying to look suitably modest as I was doing so. Then a woman came up, and she shoved a piece of paper in front of me as I was signing. She turned to all these other people and said, "Who is he? Who is he?" I thought it was good for one's soul.

Frequently during the antiapartheid struggle, those who supported the apartheid government at home would castigate me for committing what for them was the heinous crime of mixing religion with politics. They said I was a politician trying very hard to be an archbishop. Interestingly, it was those who were the privileged and who were benefiting from the unjust status code that was being condemned who took issue with me. The oppressed, in contrast, thought that perhaps I was not being political enough. The privileged were enamored of their favorite dichotomies as between the sacred and the secular, the holy and the profane, the spiritual and the material.

And yet even in this country, a land that has enshrined constitutionally the separation of church and state, it is one of the ironies of life that politicians invest considerable resources in wooing what might be regarded as influential religious constituencies, and they are scrupulous not to upset such constituencies by advocating policies that might do that in this country. There have been those who have been called the Moral Majority, who have wanted to promote a particular agenda, and so political candidates have made a point of espousing causes that would endear them to such groups. Thus politicians have known that their views on abortion or gays and lesbians were likely to alienate or win the favor of one or other religious group. If that was not mixing religion with politics, then I do not know what is. What it demonstrates is that those who do not wish to mix religion with politics are really asking for the moon. Religious faith and faith communities have for a very long time been very significant factors in public life, and those who ignore them have usually rued their stance and lived to regret it.

One of the fascinating features of human existence is the enduring characteristic of religious faith. It is something that is a given that human beings are worshiping animals. It is almost universal and as inescapable as breathing. It is part of our makeup that we must worship something or someone. It appears we are created for the transcendent, for that which is other than we are, conceived as higher, better, more intelligent, more powerful, evoking reverence of some sort and tending to drive us on to our knees. It is healthy when this other is truly transcendent, holy and good, the one whom most designate as God or the Divine. There are those who have refused to worship this one, but worship they must. They may bend their knee to something less than God, than the Divine, such as success, ambition, sex, et cetera, and almost always they are disillusioned as their god turns into dust and ashes. We are by nature religious, which does not tell us what it is that we worship or what sort of persons our worship has helped us to become.

Religious faith is resilient and not easily destroyed. Many atheistic regimes have learned to their cost that religious faith is not easy to get rid of. Frequently, the more a religion is persecuted and proscribed, the more it seems to flourish and grow. The Communist Soviet regime tried its utmost to destroy the Russian Orthodox church and other faith communities. Try as hard as it might, it had to concede defeat because, despite all the disadvantages, heaped on it as a forbidden thing, frustratingly from the atheistic government's perspective, the persecuted faiths have flourished. That seems to be the case in other places as well, such as China and elsewhere.

Religion is a potent force, but it is in fact morally mutual. It is automatically neither good nor bad. It can be either, depending on what it inspires its adherents to do. It was religious zeal that drove a Martin Luther King Jr. to struggle for justice and equity in the American civil rights movement. It was her faith that inspired Mother Teresa to expend herself so prodigally on behalf of the derelicts and the discarded of Calcutta. It is his faith that has sustained the Dalai Lama in the many years of exile from his beloved Tibet, enabling him to be one of the holiest, most serene persons I have been privileged to meet. But religion has had a malignant impact in many other situations. Those who have killed doctors who procured abortions believed they were carrying out a religious duty. Christians went on crusades to drive out the infidels from the Holy Land. Wars have flared up between adherents of the same faith in the many wars of religion that were for long a prominent feature of Europe—something that has sadly not disappeared completely as the sectarian strife in Northern Ireland shows where Christian is pitted against fellow Christian. In Iraq, the parlous situation has been exacerbated by rivalry between Sunni and Shia Muslims.

Thus, religion has the capacity to produce saints, or rogues, the perpetrators of the vilest atrocities. It really depends on what the adherent allows the religion to accomplish in him or her. This is a very important assertion, especially in our fraught days, when we so facilely speak of the war between civilizations and characterize the ghastly violence of fanatics as something somehow inherent in the faith they came to espouse, and so we slide so easily into stereotyping. Because some, perhaps many, of those who are called terrorists are Muslims, we quickly find ourselves thinking of Islam as a violent faith that eggs on its adherents to engage in acts of terror, and we end up suspecting all Arabs, and then it is soon people of Middle Eastern descent, and then any swarthy person or any stranger as we feed our growing xenophobia. Thus it was a huge shock to many Westerners when they discovered that the Bosnian Muslims looked exactly like themselves ethnically and not as they had always believed Muslims should look. It is a great tragedy when a whole religion is tarred with the same brush as that appropriate for extremist adherents of Islam. Christians would bristle with justifiable resentment if their faith was vilified by being identified with the fundamentalists who believe they are doing God's will in killing doctors who help women by procuring abortions or those others whose homophobia has led them to string up a gay man on a fence leaving him to die an excruciating death or those such as the Ku Klux Klan who believe their vile racism to be sanctioned by the Scriptures and are not ashamed to use as their particular trademark something that dishonors a symbol that Christians revere deeply, a flaming cross, when they have lynched a black man or torched his home or place of worship. We would be appalled that anyone could ever manage that these fringe groups represented mainstream Christianity.

We should be categorical and unequivocal. There is no war between people of different faiths because of the difference of faith per se. There is no war between Islam and Christianity or between Islam and Judaism. No. There are adherents of the different faiths who engage in all kinds of nefarious activities including violence and terrorism. The Oklahoma bombers were Caucasian and Christians but that did not make Christianity a violent religion that encouraged its adherents to engage in acts of terrorism. Nor can we blame Christianity for the terrible outrage in Spain just because the suspected ETA are almost all Christians. There are terrorists who happen sometimes to be Christian, sometimes Muslim, sometimes Jewish, et cetera: The cause of their terrorism lies not in their faith but in various circumstances: injustice, oppression, poverty, disease, hunger, ignorance, and so on. To combat this terrorism, we should not foolishly speak of crusades against this or that faith, but we should eradicate the root causes that can drive people to the desperation that compels them to engage in desperate acts. We will not win the war against terrorism until we do that.

The influence of faith is not only malign and baneful. No, wonderfully, it is what has been responsible for some of the most spectacular achievements of humankind. We have seen some quite awful things, and Christians need to be among the most modest because of the many ghastly things that Christians have perpetrated. We cannot be hoity-toity and speak disdainfully of "those" terrorists, many of whom have been non-Christians. After all, it has been devout Christians who are

among the most notorious slave owners, who saw no contradiction between their faith and their ownership of fellow human beings, often
fellow Christians, as if they were mere chattels and beasts of burden. It
was Christians who gave the world the horror of the Holocaust in Nazi
Germany and the excesses of fascism in Italy or Franco's Spain. It was
not pagans but Christians who found alleged biblical justification for
their injustice and inhumanity of apartheid in South Africa. It was a
Christian leader who ordered atom bombs, weapons of mass destruction, to be dropped on Hiroshima and Nagasaki on innocent, unarmed
civilians. It is Christians at one another's throats in Northern Ireland.
The Rwandan genocide happened in a land almost exclusively Christian. No, we Christians have much that should make us hang our heads
in shame. But there is much in our faith and in that of others, for which
we can be deeply thankful.

Most faiths have a very high doctrine of human beings—the Judeo
Christian faiths claiming that human beings are made in God's image
with a worth that is intrinsic and universal. It does not depend on ex-
trinsic things such as ethnicity, gender, status. It is possessed by all,
regardless of whether you are tall or short, whether you are substantial
or have an hourglass figure, whether you are beautiful or not so beautiful, whether you're rich or poor. One of the most fantastic assertions
about human beings is that you are created in the image of God, that all
of us are God's viceroys, God's stand-ins, that to treat one such as if they
were less than this is not just wrong. It is positively blasphemous for it is
almost as if you were spitting in the face of God. This imago dei is the
basis of the Universal Declaration of Human Rights and is the reason the
world stood as one in its condemnation of apartheid and all racism.

The word of God unequivocally affected the world of politics, and it
was wonderful to behold the remarkable cooperation between persons
of different faiths in our opposition to apartheid. It was one of the most
glorious moments in the history of that struggle when we were able to
walk arm in arm, Christian with Muslim with Hindu with Jew, in our
protest demonstrations against the scourge of apartheid.

Virtually all of the faiths teach fundamental moral values shared by
all: honesty, fidelity in marriage, truthfulness, courage, compassion,
concern for the other, the unity of humankind as one family, and the
value of peace. No religion teaches that it is good to steal, to lie, to be
abusive of others, to kill. They all in different ways extol peace. These

are values or ideals that world politics should strive after. These are values to inform the world of politics.

Many of the faiths exhort their adherents to be caring stewards of the rest of creation. Ecological concerns are a deeply religious, spiritual matter. To pollute the environment, to be responsible for a disastrous warming is not just wrong and should be a criminal offense; it is certainly morally wrong. It is a sin.

The faiths teach that we are ultimately family, and our destiny as the human family is in our hands as a common destiny. It is to be at odds with the precepts of most religions to be indifferent to the suffering and misery of others, to watch unconcerned when others are hungry and poor, assailed by disease and ignorance when there is much that the affluent of all faiths could do to alleviate their lot. It is obscene in the extreme to spend as much as we do on arms, on budgets of death and destruction, when, as we so well know, a small fraction of those budgets would ensure that our sisters and brothers everywhere, God's children, members of our family, would have clean water, would have enough to eat, an adequate education and health care and a decent home. We can do it if we allow our faiths to inspire us, that we are family, and in this family there are no outsiders. All belong.

Isn't it fantastic that my enemies are not God's enemies? Isn't it fantastic to know that God has no enemies, that all belong and are held in this divine embrace that leaves no one out, an embrace of love that gives up on no one, an embrace of love that will not let us go. All are held together, rich and poor, white and black, red and yellow, educated, not educated, gay, lesbian, and so-called straight.

And all faiths teach that this is a moral universe. Evil and injustice and oppression can never have the last word. Right, goodness, love, laughter, caring, sharing and compassion, peace and reconciliation will prevail over their ghastly counterparts. The powerful unjust ones who throw their weight about, who think that might is right will bite the dust and get their comeuppance. Those who rule, those who engage in politics, must know this and they must know that power is for service, not self-aggrandizement, power is for the sake of the ruled.

Mr. Secretary-General, the policies of the organization you head espouse development rather than conflict and war, the eradication of poverty, the advancement of the cause of children and women, the striving after justice and respect for the human rights of all, freedom and democracy, all these are not only sanctioned by the holy scriptures of most faiths but have the divine approval and God's blessing. Outside this building is a monument that bears the inscription to beat our swords into plowshares and our spears into pruning hooks. Your work and that of your organization, to promote global peace and harmony is a high calling, a deeply spiritual vocation, for your work is God's work.

Islam and the West

I do not believe that many issues in our world today are more pertinent than the relations between Islam and the West. I have been very much concerned with this matter during the decades I have been living in this country and even before when I lived in Iran. Why is there no symmetry in the title of the lecture? That is, why is there on the one side the word Islam, which refers to a religion, and on the other side the West, which indicates a geographical region? The response to this question, which needs another lecture to explain, reveals much about the historical development and destiny of both Islam and the West.

If there had been a United Nations six hundred years ago, when Nicholas of Cusa visited Istanbul, and there had been a discussion on this issue, the subject would have been Islam and Christendom or Islam and Christianity. Let us not forget that Islam in English has really two meanings: one is the religion of Islam and one the domain of Islam or Islamdom (if such a term were to exist, in the same way that we have Christianity and Christendom). In any case, historical developments of very different natures have caused Islam to remain Islam but Christianity or Christendom to become the West when one speaks of these two great neighboring civilizations.

Finally, let us turn to the word *and* in the title of this lecture. The word *and* not only connects A to B, it might also set A and B in opposition. The way I understand it, however, is not opposition, but instead interrelation. Today many people think that Islam and the West means Islam as opposed to the West or confronting the West. I believe that it does not have to mean the opposition of two civilizations. They have their own identities and at the same time both points of difference and points of similarity between them. And in days gone by when the West was still seen as Christendom, the similarities were greater than the differences.

Let me begin with a little bit of a historical background, because obviously we carry our history within ourselves, wherever we come from and wherever we are. One has to remember that, of course, these two civilizations, the Western, which was for a very long time a Christian civilization and still is to some extent, and the Islamic were both formed and informed by a monotheistic perspective going back to the Prophet Abraham. Moreover, a third religion, Judaism, which belongs to the same family and is of course, historically speaking, the first Abrahamic religion, played an important role in both of these civilizations. The spiritual foundation of both the West and the Islamic world is, therefore, very similar. It is true that Christianity is not Islam, and that Islam is not Christianity. There are differences, obviously, different theologies, but they are very close to each other in the most fundamental questions relating to God, the world as God's creation, the nature of the human soul, the moral character of human life, and so many other key issues.

In the fields of philosophy, logic, mathematics, and sciences such as astronomy, the two civilizations were again heir to the same intellectual universe, that of the ancient Mediterranean and especially the Hellenic and Hellenistic worlds. Moreover, the West learned much of this intellectual tradition through the Islamic world. The Islamic world was not only a transmitter of Greek ideas to the West, but also the creator of many new ideas also transmitted to the West. If St. Thomas Aquinas and Avicenna had sat down together, they would have been able to have a discourse based on much mutual understanding, precisely because they belonged to similar universes of intellectual understanding.

Despite the fact, however, that both the religious and intellectual foundations of the West and the Islamic world are very close together, historically, these worlds did not develop in the same way. The reasons are manifold and cannot be discussed here. But, as an example, the Islamic world captured very rapidly the southern part of the Mediterranean Sea, forced European civilization northward, and was for a long time a threat to the very existence of the West, that is, of western Europe, of which America is an heir. The threat from the West to the Islamic world, however, did not exist in the Middle Ages. It came much later, in the modern colonial period. Every civilization sees some other society as "the other." For Islamic civilization, there were several others. Islam knew Hindu and Buddhist India, Confucian and Taoist China, not to mention Zoroastrian Persia. Muslims also knew non-Islamic and non-Christian black Africa. There were, moreover, Muslims in the Malay world who encountered earlier Hindu societies in Java and Sumatra. In all these worlds, the Muslims encountered many others, though they faced more directly the Byzantine and the eastern European world as well as western Europe as others that were Christian. But none of these others threatened the existence of Islam in its early history.

Western Europe, however, was confronted and even threatened by only one power, the Islamic world. Islam was the most significant and only non-Christian other it knew. Thus the idea so deeply and profoundly embedded in the Western psyche of the other, for a long time a threatening other, was the Islamic world. That has had and continues to have very unfortunate consequences for our own world.

Furthermore, Christianity, as the major religion of the West, had never been threatened or questioned by any religious force except Islam. And, because Christ is the central figure of Christianity, Islam came to be identified by many Christians in the Middle Ages and even later with the Antichrist. Given that Christ was the central figure of Christianity, people in the West believed that because the Prophet of Islam occupied the same central position in Islam, if they could turn him into a demonic figure they would destroy Islam. Therefore, the attacks against Islam in Europe during the Middle Ages and even later were mostly desecration of the personality of the Prophet. This is exactly what we hear in many quarters today. History is in a sense repeating itself. But then, as now, most people did not understand that Islam is based on the Oneness of God and not on any prophetic figure.

The Prophet is a conveyor of a message from God and God is the central reality of Islam. This is why from the Islamic point of view it is religiously false and theologically absurd to call Islam Muhammadanism. In any case, insults against the Prophet in the West go back to the Middle Ages and are a major stumbling block for better relations between Islam and the West.

Another major word that has led to so much misunderstanding and, when misused, so much harm is *jihad.* One of the great paradoxes of our time is that people speak all the time about jihad in a pejorative way with no sense of its original meaning as striving (for the cause of God). Even some Muslims misconstrue and misuse and even abuse the term. The sad fact is that many people, especially in the West, now use *jihad* in titles of their books so that more readers will purchase a copy. But the word *jihad* first appeared in the pages of Western books in the wake of the Crusades, themselves a Western jihad against Islam. The idea of crusade followed by the action of crusading was central to the medieval European mind. Jihad, on the other hand, usually mistranslated as holy war, was often seen in the West as being both a characteristic of Islam and a response to the Crusades. Nor have crusading and jihad in reaction to each other been lost in the modern world. All one has to do is to remember the recent Western invasion of Iraq. In any case, in thinking about the theme of Islam and the West the interplay and interaction between the concepts of crusade and jihad are important to keep in mind.

It needs to be added that historically the Crusades became a defining moment only for the eastern Arab part of the Islamic world in its relation to the West. I am Persian by origin, and my father was born in Kashan in central Iran. In that city even today few among the common people have even heard of the Crusades, whose influence did not get that far in the Islamic world. For Europe, however, the Crusades marked a profound transformation that was followed after the end of the Middle Ages by aggressive proselytizing in the name of Christianity or, later, secularized Western values in other societies and cultures, including of course the Islamic. Furthermore, since the seventeenth century, the theater of Western crusading has been various Islamic lands. The reverse, however, has not been true until very recently, when terrorists from the Islamic world claiming to be carrying out jihad, but doing so without attention to conditions that Islamic law has established for it as a struggle to defend Islam and the Islamic world, have been taken to the West.

Turning to the more general attitude of the West toward the Islamic world, we can see a paradoxical situation in the Middle Ages. On the one hand, there was a great deal of respect for Islamic civilization, and many Europeans even learned Arabic to master Islamic science from mathematics to astronomy to medicine to alchemy. Arabic texts were translated into Latin and Islamic philosophy was finally taught in Paris after having been forbidden. On the other hand, there was strident opposition to Islam as a religion viewed as a heresy to be opposed and feared. This ambivalent attitude gave way in the Renaissance to simply disdain for Islam and its civilization and, unfortunately, it is this latter attitude that has remained in the consciousness of Western people to this day and still colors the attitude of most Westerners toward Islam.

An important and often-forgotten point is that during the entire period leading up to the modern era, from the expulsion of Muslims from Spain and the European colonization of much of the Islamic world, throughout many Muslim countries Christians and Jews lived among the Muslims, usually in peace. In fact, many Jews took refuge in Islamic lands after their expulsion from Europe. The negative relations and attitudes between Muslims and Jews today are modern phenomena resulting from the rise of Zionism, the partition of Palestine in 1948, and its aftermath.

In the classical Islamic world one sees, for example, Jewish poets who wrote in Arabic or Persian or composed poetry in Hebrew based on Islamic models. In Persia, Iraq, Syria, Egypt, Yemen, and Morocco, Christians were artists and craftsmen and played a role in many different facets of the cultural life of the Islamic society in which they lived. In the seventeenth century, Jewish ministers served in the Ottoman Court and many bankers in Istanbul were Jewish. There have in fact always been many Jewish merchants in various Islamic countries. Historically there has been no parallelism between Islamic attitudes toward Judaism and Christianity and Western attitudes toward Islam.

There is another important reality to consider. During the classical and premodern periods of Islamic and Western civilizations, the Islamic world had no fear of the West, but the West did have a fear of the Islamic world. In fact, the Muslims made the great mistake, when the colonial onslaught occurred, of not fearing the power of the West early enough. When the Portuguese and the Dutch began to cut away at one of the main economic lifelines of Islamic civilization in the sixteenth century by dominating navigation of the Indian Ocean, the heart of the Islamic world did not realize what had happened to it. It still had the land trade route, the Silk Road, going from China to Syria and finally to Venice and other European cities. It took a couple of centuries for the heartland of the Islamic world to realize that it was now facing a mortal danger from the West. That awareness came both symbolically and in actuality with the Napoleonic invasion of Egypt in 1798. A French general of slight build named Napoleon Bonaparte destroyed the remnants of the once mighty Mamluk army, decimating it near the pyramids in just one day, and with that victory Mamluk power, which a few centuries earlier had finally stopped the devastating Mongol invasion from the East, came to an end, and the West succeeded in dominating over a major country at the heart of the Islamic world.

The fear of the West in the Islamic world, then, began with the Napoleonic invasion of Egypt, whereas the fear of the Islamic world in the West goes back to a much earlier formative period in its own history and therefore persists paradoxically to this day, when the West exercises such overwhelming military and economic superiority over the Islamic world. The West speaks of having interest in this or that part of the Islamic areas, whereas Muslims can never even speak, not to mention take action, about their interests in the Western world. Whatever appearances may or may not be, there is no doubt that many Islamic countries still live under some form of neocolonialism, even as many in the West still speak of fear of domination of the West by Islam in order to create hatred against Muslims while in reality exercising so much domination over them.

After the Napoleonic invasion of Egypt in 1798, that country became a colony, as did India after the 1857 revolt in Delhi against the British. Many parts of Islamic Africa were colonized by the British and the French, and Central Asia was by the Russians. The parts of the Islamic world that remained nominally free during the colonial period were some of the lands at the center, including the Ottoman territory, Persia, Afghanistan, and the center of Arabia. But even in those states there was great pressure from Western powers and much negative influence. Consequently, many elements of Islamic society crumbled from within, including many of its civilizational and cultural institutions, though these external forces were not able to destroy the Islamic religion itself. The faith of the people survived despite the colonial experience and in fact has remained strong and has even revived.

Political independence came to most Islamic countries after World War II, but cultural and economic domination of the Islamic world by the West continued. Most Muslims had great hope that with political independence would come the revival of Islamic civilization, culture, education, and law, but this did not happen to any appreciable degree. In many domains, the invasion of the Islamic world by forces of secularism issuing from the West actually intensified.

From that time on, various forms of resistance and opposition to these forces arose and a new malaise set in many Islamic lands. This malaise should have been able to express itself through normal political processes in Islamic society except that such processes were neither in place nor possible in most Islamic countries, which were autocratic, outwardly nationalistic, and local cultures but in reality Westernized elites supported by Western powers with different political and economic interests. There was no space or time for the inner forces of Islamic society to work themselves out through a natural process. This situation contributed to extremism and violence, which have led today to upheavals from civil strife and military uprisings by major groups to desperate acts of terrorism by marginal groups. Few Western analysts have been willing to consider the deeper reasons for these reactions, content to speak simply of Islamic terrorism, which serves their political agendas. What is called Islamic terrorism today is in fact a misnomer. Protestants and Catholics, for example, killed each other, including innocent people, in Ireland for a long time, just as Jews bomb the civilian Palestinian population, but few speak of Christian or Jewish terrorism.

Today, many people in the West assert that the Islamic world is anti-Western, but this is not generally true. The vast majority of Muslims are not anti-Western but instead against Western interests in the Islamic world that conflict with Islamic interests. If the Islamic world could be left alone to develop its own resources, to respond to its own inner call, to answer in a creative way to the tension that exists there today between traditional norms and modern ideas, there would not be opposition to the West. Many Muslims do oppose Western norms being imposed upon them but do not oppose the West for being Western within Western borders. Muslims do not want to dictate to Swedes or

Americans how they should conduct their lives. They are opposed to the West only inasmuch as it wants to dictate to Muslims how they should live theirs.

There is no anti-Japanism in Indonesia today. Yes, the Indonesians were very anti-Japanese during World War II, when they were occupied by Japan. At that time there was a very good reason for their anti-Japanese attitude but that reason no longer exists.

The Iranians have never been anti-Japanese because they were never occupied by Japan. Today they trade with Japan and a great deal of technology comes from Japan into Iran, Syria, and elsewhere in the Islamic world. Many Muslims have become anti-Western because they see their governments, often supported by the West, taking away their freedoms, shoving down their throat ideas, norms, arts, cinema, music, social ideas, and so forth, which they do not feel to be their own but Western in origin.

There is today in the Islamic world a great desire and much effort to better understand the West more than there is in the West a desire or effort to understand the Islamic world. But parallel with that tendency is also a kind of closing of doors. When a being is threatened externally, usually, like a turtle, it goes inside its shell. The threat to the identity of the Islamic world and its distinct culture and even religion has caused many Muslims to retreat more and more into their shells intellectually and culturally, which leads then to their becoming more exclusive, and even against what traditional Islam had always stood for—namely, an openness to other religions and cultures.

There is no doubt that, although so many elements of Western origin from technology to political ideas continue to spread among Muslims, this sense of wanting to go into one's own shell is a pronounced tendency within the Islamic world today. But just as strong is the other tendency of wanting to come out even more and, while preserving their Islamic identity, to embrace and espouse with open arms other worldviews and especially to better understand other religions, especially Christianity.

Unfortunately, despite the increase of knowledge on both sides about the other, there is also a kind of complementary action and reaction between Islam and the West that is far from positive. Every form of exclusivism that in the Islamic world has its mirror image in the West, including the United States, and vice versa. In Europe, religion is too weak for religious exclusivists to have their voice heard, but cultural exclusivism combined with what is called Islamophobia today, is prevalent and on the increase. When only 9 percent of people in France go to church, what a Catholic theologian says does not have the same impact as what a Protestant minister says in Georgia, South Carolina, or Tennessee.

Now, those who are fair-minded and moderates in both the West and the Islamic world and who seek earnestly mutual peace and understanding have to speak loudly enough to drown out the message of hatred, mutual vilification, and blind exclusivism that has become so prevalent on both sides. But that is difficult because the message of peace and mutual understanding does not sell as well in the media as that of hatred and incitement to violence. People working quietly and in peace for better understanding do not, unfortunately, receive the same kind of media coverage as apostles of hate. The truth is, that the deep need and desire for mutual understanding between Islam and the West has never been greater than it is now, when the danger of clash and mutual destruction has also never been greater.

The Islamic world cannot isolate itself from the West, nor can the West isolate itself from the Islamic world. The destiny of all of us depends on the way in which we are able to create not mutual confrontation and hatred, but instead mutual respect, understanding, and complementarity between our two great civilizations. I hope that in this august body—and this is the most important body in this country and in the world for this task—an atmosphere will be created in which vilification and opposition will give way to trust, respect, and understanding. There is no other way to attain peace. The era of domination of one side by the other is over and the sooner everyone, especially the strong, realizes this truth, the better it is for humanity as a whole. Whether we like it or not, the destinies of Islam and the West are intertwined.

IV.

Science and Technology

9

Designer Genes:
The Ethics of Modern Genetics

ERIC WIESCHAUS

It is obviously a pleasure and a great honor for me to come here today to talk to you about science.

I am going to talk to you from a very personal perspective. I am still at this age a practicing scientist. I go into the lab every day, spend four, five hours at the bench, doing my own experiments. The practice of science and the ability to do science and react to one's own experimental results has shaped me as a person, and also therefore shaped how I think about many of the major ethical and social issues we confront today.

This afternoon I would like to share some of my personal experience as a scientist with you, and for me to do that I will have to train you a little bit as scientists. I must warn you that a significant part of the first minutes of this lecture is going to be about DNA, and about embryonic development, because I think it is important for you to understand the facts of the science if you are going to be able to understand how a scientist develops an ethical perspective about these issues.

We live in what could be called the era of modern genetics. You all know that the human genome, human DNA, has been now completely sequenced. You know that there are about thirty thousand different genes. Each of those genes encodes a protein and there are thirty thousand different proteins that humans can make. These numbers influence how I think about the problem of development. What basically has to happen in each embryo is that individual cells must give rise to a whole variety of cell types—muscle cells, eye cells, skin cells. The embryo does this by having individual cells begin to express different genes. The reason that the muscle cells are muscle cells is that they express particular muscle genes. Your eye cells, on the other hand, express genes that are characteristic of eyes. The central problem in understanding how embryos develop is that all of the cells in your body have the same DNA; they all have the same genes and the capacity to make the same proteins. Cells differentiate and form organs because they choose to use only a subset of those genes. But how are these choices made? Why does one cell use muscle genes and become muscle and other cells use other genes? And when do these choices become irreversible?

The techniques of molecular biology developed over the past twenty years have transformed our ability to ask these questions. We now understand more about the development of embryos and the way genes control that development than we ever did or ever imagined we would. This is in large part because molecular technologies let us see individual gene products and follow them in living embryos.

A large amount of work over the past twenty years can be summed up in terms of two really basic understandings that are central to our thinking about embryos. The first is that the patterns of gene activity in embryos are extremely transient and change constantly. Sometimes over five- to ten-minute periods a cell will express a gene, turn that gene off, express another gene, turn that gene off, express another gene. Embryonic development therefore is characterized by constant change in gene activities.

It is very different than what we know about the gene activities in adults. Our skin cells stay and function as skin cells because those cells continue to express the same gene, and it is that stability of gene expression in the nucleus of skin cells that allows those cells to function, to do particular jobs in our body. It is the reason we survive as adults. We do not want our skin cells suddenly changing gene expression and turning into eyes. So cells in an adult have extremely stable patterns of gene expression, and that is very different from what we see in embryos.

A second major conclusion, drawn from many experiments, is that the patterns of gene activity you see in embryos are not there from the beginning, but instead are derived and developed by the cells in the embryo through signals that cells send to one another.

It is very much, if you will, as if the communication itself gives rise to the pattern and order in an embryo. I imagine this is not very different from what happens in any human organization where consensus and a group plan arises through conversation, through signals, through a certain degree of competition between cells to assume specific roles, and a certain ability of cells to perceive what other cells have done and to make their choices accordingly. Cells of course use chemicals rather than words to accomplish this communication, but the basic process is very similar.

The dependence on this cell communication means that embryonic patterns arise gradually and are flexible, and represents almost a self-organizing property the cells possess because they are members of a group. The capacity of cells to self-organize is probably one of the things that fascinate us most as scientists—we want to understand how it is that a group of cells, through communication, can organize themselves reliably into the same increasingly complex patterns. You could take any two embryos at this early stage and fuse them together, and they would make one embryo. You could also take them and divide them in half and form smaller groups of cells, but the smaller groups would still be able to self-organize into a perfect embryo.

That flexibility of embryonic cells has allowed scientists in the past ten to twenty years to establish what are called embryonic stem cells in culture dishes. To isolate such stem cells from the embryo, you take away the part that is going to form the trophectoderm or placenta and put the cells into a Petri dish. Because these cells are so flexible and because they are not programmed to make anything in particular, you can grow them for a long time, maintain them in culture, and study them. These cultured cells are capable of forming muscle cells or skin cells or nerve cells. They therefore offer a great potential for scientists to study the development of cells and how cells achieve their individual characteristics. Cultured embryonic stem cells would also obviously offer great clinical potential as well, if we scientists were able to control in culture the cell communication processes that determine how cells achieve their individual characteristics.

It is very difficult—possibly even impossible—to duplicate all of the properties of embryonic stem cells using other cell types. The same feature of the adult cells, of the nuclei of these adult cells—which make gene expression so stable and allow the cells to function as well as skin or eyes—keep them from showing the flexibility required to establish cultures from them. Even the dividing stem cell systems in our skin, our liver, the blood cells, those cells that allow us to maintain those structures in the adult, as far as we can see as scientists, are more restricted in their potential than embryonic cells.

A major challenge for scientists is to develop strategies to establish cell cultures comparable to embryonic stem cells from adults. There are a number of good scientific reasons why you might want to do this. For example, even when different adults develop a very similar form of cancer, the individual tumors are in fact very different and every tumor has a different history. You might want to compare the cells of different tumors. To do this, you would need to grow them in culture without subjecting them to any major change. Converting the adult differentiated tumor cells into embryonic stem cells might be one way. There also might be therapeutic uses for stem cells if they could be established from an adult patient. For example, you might want to match donor cells with a patient suffering from a particular disease. However, the stability of gene expression pattern in the nuclei of adult differentiated cells makes these types of experiments very difficult.

There is one strategy for reversing that stable differentiation of the nuclei. The technique scientists have developed is called somatic nuclear transfer, and is based on the idea that there must be something in the egg that allows the DNA and the nucleus of that egg cell to be very flexible. If you could take adult cells and expose them to that mysterious something, you might be able to have the nuclei of those adult cells regaining their flexibility, a flexibility that would allow you to establish cells from the new culture.

Simply grinding up eggs and throwing them on to a Petri dish where you put adult cells has not worked. Something in those egg cells is important, and somatic nuclear transfer provides one strategy to expose these adult nuclei to the cytoplasm of an egg. The process starts with an unfertilized egg and a differentiated cell that you wanted to establish a culture from. You remove the nucleus and the DNA from the unfertilized egg, and you introduce the nucleus of the adult cell into the environment of that unfertilized egg. That introduction is enough to release the restrictive program on that adult cell nucleus and to allow it to divide. This process allows you to establish cultures from adult cells that have the same potential previously seen only in embryonic stem cells.

We know this strategy works effectively on a variety of known embryos. It has not yet been used on human cells; however, it has evoked a great deal of controversy. I have chosen to talk about somatic nuclear transfer partly because I am aware of the discussion in the press recently and also because it provides a good example of how scientists may see a process differently than the public does. Somatic nuclear transfer is controversial because it uses human eggs and because certain aspects of the process are similar to normal human development.

In normal human development, an unfertilized egg is fertilized by a single sperm, and after that fertilization each egg will divide to produce a ball of cells that will form trophectoderm and an inner cell mass, eventually implanting itself into the wall of the uterus and continuing development as an embryo. It is after implantation has occurred that the self-organizing properties in the embryo are thought to give rise to the primitive streak.

In almost all human society, the crucial first step in this sequence is regarded as fertilization, largely because fertilization brings together the DNA of the egg and the sperm. The nucleus formed by this process has a new combination of DNA. We have learned from the human gene project that there are enough differences in genes among human beings that every sperm and every egg is different and thus every embryo formed by fertilization has a different genotype. The fusion of egg and sperm DNA from two individuals makes fertilization an important step in what otherwise, from a scientific standpoint, one would consider a continuous process.

Although some of the images look the same, somatic nuclear transfer is something different. There is no fusion of egg and sperm to create a new genotype. Instead, what we have done is taken an older nucleus—the nucleus of an adult cell—and put it into an egg environment and allowed that nucleus to divide. Thus, somatic nuclear transfer does not establish a new genotype. Instead, by exposing a nucleus to the cytoplasm of the egg, it prolongs the life of that nucleus, giving it the potential to be maintained in culture. For that reason, many scientists make an ethical distinction between somatic nuclear transfer to establish cell cultures and a fertilization that would lead to a genetically distinct individual and normal embryonic development.

One of the issues that complicates many policy discussions (and many scientific discussions as well) is the mixing of phenomena that are really very different. Reproductive cloning, normal fertilization, embryonic development, somatic nuclear transfer, and embryonic stem cells all involve the use of eggs and DNA and certain aspects of cell division and early development, but scientists see them as different phenomena. Each raises different ethical issues and merits their own separate ethical discussion.

One of the difficulties in ethical evaluations of somatic nuclear transfer and embryonic stem cells is defining when individual life begins in what looks like a very continuous process. It might seem natural to assume that such individuality begins at fertilization, because it is the time where two different DNAs come together to form a new genotype. Such a criterion would be difficult to apply to somatic nuclear transfer because it does not involve fertilization. Besides, it seems to me one could argue that a new combination of genes in the nucleus does not mean that the fertilized egg is an individual, largely because it is not our own unique genotypes that define our personhood. A fertilized egg does not always give rise to a single individual. Identical twins arise from fertilized eggs that, rather than giving rise to a single embryo, in the process of organization in these late stages, sometimes happen to organize themselves into two groups and establish two axes, two embryos, give rise to identical twins. Those two identical twins came from the same fertilization event and are genetically identical, and yet in all societies we regard them as being separate and distinct individuals.

The ability of multiple fertilized eggs to form a single individual and of a single fertilized egg to form multiple individuals arise from the unprogrammed nature of early embryonic cells and their dependence on cell communication and self-organization for setting up patterns.

If our individuality is not immediately related to the chance event of fertilization, then it must arise at some point during the process of embryonic development. If it depends on self-organization, then the really essential question for scientists (and I think also for society) is to determine when this self-organization process is advanced enough that the embryos become a person. This is, however, not a question that science can actually answer. It can tell you how things happen, but it cannot tell you when an embryo becomes a person because personhood is a property, a quality that human society as a whole has to define.

I have subjected you to this enormous amount of science and certainly more science than you anticipated on coming into this room, because I believe that an understanding of science and especially the science of embryonic development should have an impact in how we as a society discuss these issues: the issues of reproductive cloning, the issues of therapeutic cloning, and of embryonic stem cells. I am struck sometimes by the difference between the way scientists discuss these issues and the way the general public does. Scientists, particularly those working in the field, have discussed and argued the science over the past twenty years and gradually come to a common accepted view on what happened in an embryo. Based on that common perception, it has been possible for the American Society of Cell Biologists and the National Academy [of Sciences] to come up with a consensus view, one that makes a clear distinction between therapeutic cloning, somatic nuclear transfer, and reproductive cloning.

But not everyone is a scientist and I do not believe that the ethical views of scientists carry any special weight. Mankind has survived a long time on this earth not knowing any of the science that I told you about today. Besides, all science has a certain level of uncertainty. It is possible to imagine in the next hundred years, scientists looking back at us at this century and smiling at the level of our misunderstanding of some of the experiments, of some of the facts of DNA. And yet we all know the great value that science has brought to human society in spite of this uncertainty.

Our natural response to this uncertainty has always been our religious and cultural traditions that give us the strength to confront the eternal issues of life and death, and war and peace on this earth. These cultural traditions are founded in our histories and reflect an understanding of the world gained in previous generations. New scientific advances often come in conflict with those previous understandings. Because both scientific advances and cultural traditions have been and continue to be so valuable to us, we have as an obligation somehow to integrate the science that we learn each day with the great values of our cultural traditions.

This has been the history of almost all science and the history of human life—the interaction between our cultural and religious traditions and new scientific discoveries that seem to conflict with them. It almost always happens that those conflicts turn out to be not real. There is no absolute conflict between them.

The only way that we can integrate scientific discoveries and our cultural traditions is, I think, to discuss the science as well as the social and ethical issues.

10

Genetically Modified Crops for Developed Countries

DAPHNE PREUSS AND JENNIFER THOMSON

Daphne Preuss

Over the past decade, we have witnessed the broad introduction of a new type of agricultural technology—the development of food varieties often described as genetically modified (GM). I will describe the science behind this technology, the potential benefits and risks, and the challenges for policymakers who wish to ensure developing countries have access to the technology.

My research at the University of Chicago focuses on understanding inheritance in plants. We work on pollination and on DNA transmission, all in a rapidly growing weed that is useful for genetic studies.

According to the World Health Organization, malnutrition is the leading cause of death worldwide. More than 170 million children are underweight, and in developing countries, 3 million children die each year from malnutrition. Worldwide, food production must increase by as much as 25 percent to keep pace with population growth; in developing countries, larger increases will be required to avoid added reliance on imports.

Over the past decades, vast tracts of uncultivated land have been converted into production; even so, less than 11 percent of the world's surface is well suited to agriculture. As the population increases, there will not be enough land available to meet food requirements—finding ways to enable plants to grow on compromised soils is the most effective means available for meeting these growing demands.

All organisms have tremendous genetic diversity within their populations; humans learned long ago to use selective breeding to capture this diversity and to enhance desirable traits. We are all familiar with the extraordinary changes that took place in the domestication of animals; perhaps less familiar is the similar selection process that led to the domestication of all of our major crops. Just ten thousand years ago, the plant known as maize looked very different; called *teosinte*, it produced only very few seeds, each encased in a tough shell, and scattered onto the soil. Changes in only five genes, discovered by people living in Central and South America, led to the development of maize as we now know it.

Similar changes occurred in all our major food crops. Selective breeding identified a mixture of three grass genomes, leading to wheat; breeding also reduced the toxicity of natural potatoes. These changes were slow initially, but with the advent of modern genetics one hundred years ago, their pace accelerated. Considered merely an extension of conventional breeding, crops were altered by making random mutations, creating hybrids, culturing tissues and fusing embryos. In the past decade, a new technology—molecular biology—has been applied, sparking concerns where few had been previously raised.

One concern is that conventional methods primarily combine genes from plants, typically of the same species, whereas recombinant DNA methods can employ a gene derived from any organism. While this may sound particularly unnatural, the results of the genome sequencing projects have shown us that all organisms have many genes in common—in fact, approximately half of the genes in a plant genome are also found in the human genome. It is not at all clear whether there is an added risk associated with introducing a gene from a nonplant species—after all, many plants we eat were once toxic and half of all natural chemicals are carcinogens; consequently, genes derived from a plant are not always harmless.

Even with the capability to move genes between species, many of the changes made by genetic engineering are much more subtle, as demonstrated in the discovery of genes that allow plants to grow on salty soil. Salt contamination eliminates large quantities of land from production, yet traditional breeding has made little progress in increasing the tolerance of plants to salt. Increasing the levels of a naturally occurring salt pump within plant cells allows them to grow in otherwise lethal salt concentrations. In other cases of genetic engineering, it is desirable to decrease the levels of a natural gene, removing a product that is ordinarily in the plant. Such changes would appear to pose little concern from a safety standpoint.

It is also useful to enable a plant to perform a chemical step that may have been eliminated by the centuries of selective breeding. For example, some plants can convert vegetable oil to castor oil by the modification of a particular carbon, yet many of our crops have lost this ability. Moving the relevant gene into a target plant makes it possible to perform a precise chemical reaction. Using plants as chemical factories is a very promising application, potentially increasing supplies with minimal creation of toxic pollutants. There are many other applications of GM technologies—these examples illustrate the enormous potential of this technology for the production of a wide range of beneficial products.

As with any technology, there are inherent risks to developing GM food. Genes that are helpful or harmful could be added, and tests need to be in place to determine the consequences. We must ask whether the gene harms humans, animals, or insects, and whether it is harmful to the environment. While fairly simple methods can be used to quantify most of these risks, the question of allergenicity is more difficult, given the relatively low probability of allergic responses in a population. In all cases, these risks are not novel; they are often higher when foods are developed using techniques that fall under the scope of conventional breeding. Such breeding techniques randomly scramble two genomes, mixing at least twenty-five thousand genes. In many cases, one or both of the genomes has been treated to generate mutations, and in subsequent generations, the desirable change is followed, but the presence of other changes is not tracked. The hybridization of two species, a process considered natural by many, is fraught with even more uncertainty. In contrast, the addition of a gene with GM technology is less dramatic. More important, it is possible to have defined knowledge of the alteration that was made. Consequently, because it is possible to perform defined tests, GM foods are likely to be even safer than conventional varieties.

When faced with a new development, how do we best consider the risks? One method is to compare the new technology with current practices. For example, here in the United States, the introduction of the biological pesticide Bt into cotton significantly reduced chemical pesticide spraying. These chemicals are harmful to animals and humans, and the biological pesticide is far more specific. Similar comparisons should be made when new GM foods are introduced: we need to take into account the current practices and their associated risks.

As GM food technology has developed, it has come under fire from several quarters; the concerns raised have prompted the development of new products that alleviate many of those concerns. The enormous flexibility of GM technology, and the fairly rapid time to move new developments to the marketplace makes this technology ideal for responding to demands and concerns expressed by consumers. As this technology goes forward, it is important to balance the concerns of many parties and to develop the technology in a manner that supports a sustainable environment. Attention to regulatory burdens and intellectual property laws is needed in order to ensure that developing countries have ready access to food. At the same time, it is important for industrialized countries to develop incentives that ensure advances that will increase food availability.

Jennifer Thomson

When I am interviewed on radio on this subject, the talk show host often asks me at the end, "Why are you so passionate about this subject?" Well, maybe for two reasons. First, I work in the field myself. I work on genetically modified maize to develop drought tolerance and resistance to African endemic viruses. But, even more important, I have seen the effect it has had on the lives of small-scale farmers in many countries, but, most important, in my own country, South Africa. I make no apologies for being passionate about the subject, but I hope I will bring my scientific expertise to point out the checks and the balances that we have to take into account.

I start with the green revolution because it made such an important impact on agricultural practices, although not so much in Africa. It did rely on new breeds of crops, but it also required the use of fertilizers. Countries like Mexico became self-sufficient in maize, but there has been less success in Africa, partly because many of our farmers cannot afford the use of a fertilizer. In Africa, yields have not changed in forty years, and, in fact, cereal production per capita has been steadily declining. In the words of the president of the Rockefeller Foundation, "What we need now, if we are going to feed the world, is a doubly green revolution." And GM crops are only part, but an important part, of the doubly green revolution.

If one considers the projected cereal yields in the year 2025, the shortfalls, using current agricultural practices, are going to be nearly 90 million tons of cereal in sub-Saharan Africa and higher in various other parts of the world. We are going to have to do something about improving our technology.

If we look at the power of genetic modification, we could begin to harvest marginal land through drought tolerance, increased productivity, and disease and pest resistance. But the important thing about GM technology is it gives us access to a broader gene pool than just plants. And a lot of farmers around the world are seeing the benefit of this technology. But I must hasten to say that in developing countries many people will ask, "But what's the benefit to the consumer?" Do not forget that in many developing countries the consumer is also the farmer. Many of the traits that have been used, introduced into crops, allow farmers to manage their crops better and in a much safer way for the environment.

There is also increased productivity and a decrease in health hazards. And because developing countries are using fewer pesticides, and they are more biodegradable herbicides, they are getting a safer environment.

But does this technology benefit the poor? I believe it certainly does. Now let me give you an example that I know very well from my own country, the impact of insect-resistant cotton and maize in South Africa. I was involved in the first trials that small-scale farmers in the province of KwaZulu-Natal undertook in 1997. In that year, we managed to persuade four farmers to participate in these trials. Their profits were so much increased that year that very soon their neighbors were taking part. Five years later, more than two thousand small-scale farmers in KwaZulu-Natal were planting commercially available insect-resistant cotton.

Because we are not spraying with insecticides to the same extent, we are getting an increase in nontarget insects, many of which are beneficial. There is a decrease in human insecticide poisoning. With GM technology, the cutting down in spraying has dramatic effects. Uganda, a couple of years ago, nearly lost its entire cassava crop to the African cassava mosaic virus. These plants have nothing to defend themselves, but we can give them something because of GM technology. Golden rice is nutrient enriched. The grains are slightly more golden than the parental because the genes that enable the plant—the rice—to produce the precursor of vitamin A were taken from a daffodil. So they have turned the rice slightly yellow. They are also enriched with iron, which means that people who rely entirely on rice for their diet and are subject to huge problems of vitamin A deficiency can obtain them using golden rice.

Now, just briefly on food safety issues, because this has been a topic of considerable interest on my continent. No food in the history of humankind has ever been treated as if it were a toxin other than food derived from genetically modified crops. Ninety-day, standard toxicological animal trials at very high doses, which are predictive for long-term safety, have only been tested on genetically modified foods or foods derived from genetically modified crops. So, if you were to ask me, "How do you know this food is safe?" I would say, "The only food that I know is safe is that derived from genetically modified crops because that is the only food that has been tested in this way."

Environmental safety issues are, however, of more interest to me because I think we need to be doing studies on a long-term basis on a very broad scale on a case-by-case basis. We do not want herbicide-resistant genes to be transferred to weedy relatives. We do not want to have what the press calls super-weeds developing. We do not want our insects to become resistant to the Bt toxin that gives the plants insect resistance. What about pollen spread and gene flow, and what are the consequences? These need to be studied. What about horizontal gene transfer? Vertical gene transfer is from parent to offspring; horizontal is from one organism to another. Can this occur? If it occurs, what are the consequences? Will this result in an increase in antibiotic resistance?

As regards regulatory issues, genetically modified organisms are used only in a few countries in Africa because biosafety regulations must be in place before they can use such crops. The United Nations Environmental Program, together with the global environmental facility, has set up a biosafety project. The aim is to assist up to one hundred countries over the next two to three years to develop national biosafety frameworks. So, among other things, they can comply with the Cartagena Protocol and transport or movement of GM crops. This is a very worthwhile enterprise.

In conclusion, I would say that, amongst scientists who have studied this area, there is consensus that the foods derived from GM crops are safe. That does not mean we will not continue to monitor, and it does not mean that we can sit back on our laurels. However, the environmental impacts still need to be addressed on a case-by-case basis—things like potential weediness, insect-resistance, and pollen spread. But, in every case, we have to look at the risks and we have to weigh out the benefits, and we also have to look at the risks of not embarking on a technology.

I have vivid memories of being a postdoctorate fellow at Harvard in 1974, the year genetic engineering started, and the lobby to stop it dead in its tracks was very powerful.

In 1974, we did not know AIDS existed. We did not know the HIV virus existed. If the lobby had been successful to stop genetic engineering dead in its tracks, we would never have a hope of a vaccine for HIV/AIDS. Similarly, we do not know now what environmental perturbations are going to happen in the next couple of decades. If we are to stop GM technology for crops, we may be losing out on a potential saving technology.

V.

United Nations

11

Act of Creation:
The Founding of the United Nations

STEPHEN SCHLESINGER

I would like to thank Secretary-General Kofi Annan very much for that extremely kind introduction. I am very pleased and very honored to be here today.

This is really a very nice occasion to talk about where this great organization originally came from. I will talk today about how the UN charter came into being at the 1945 conference in San Francisco. It was there, as you may recall, that some fifty countries gathered to draft this landmark document that set up this institution in order to guarantee peace around the world.

It is this subject about which I have written my book, *Act of Creation*. Frankly, at the time, I thought I would be relating a very familiar story. But I soon found out in the course of my research, that there had been no full study of that extraordinary conclave. Somehow, over time, the UN's creation had begun simply to be taken for granted by its membership, indeed by the world.

However, as we all know, history is to civilization as memory is to the individual. We really do need to know where we have come from.

The more knowledge we have about the UN's origins, the better ability we will have to improve and strengthen the organization for the future. This was the real impetus behind my own quest to seek out what had happened in San Francisco.

Now, in the establishment of any large global body, there are always going to be many framers, many authors, many parents. This was certainly true of the birthing story of the United Nations. But if there was one single individual and one single state to whom we can attribute much of this singular accomplishment, it was surely to President Franklin Roosevelt and the United States.

Understanding this reality, I tell this tale mainly from the American viewpoint.

Franklin Roosevelt, indeed, was the central figure in this drama. Above all, he was the one who drove the idea forward with his signature flair and his iron determination. As many of you may know, he began his career as the assistant secretary of the Navy under President Woodrow Wilson. It was there that he became a fervent supporter of Wilson's dream of establishing a League of Nations following the end of World War I.

Wilson's plan really drew on our common geopolitical heritage, starting with the Peace of Westphalia in 1648 after the Thirty Years War and the Congress of Vienna in 1815, after the Napoleonic wars. Along with the concept developed in the eighteenth century by the great philosopher Immanuel Kant in his treatise "Perpetual Peace." In simplest terms, Wilson proposed a global assembly that would bring together all nations under international law in peaceable relations.

As a mark of his commitment, Franklin Roosevelt delivered hundreds of speeches around the United States in 1919 and 1920 in favor of the organization. But he was bitterly disappointed when the measure to join went down in defeat in the U.S. Senate, meaning that the United States would never join the organization and dealing the League of Nations a blow from which it never fully recovered. But Roosevelt had learned very valuable lessons on how to avoid the pitfalls of setting up a similar type of organization in the future.

It was in 1939, seven years after his accession to the presidency, that Roosevelt saw the war clouds gathering in Europe and became convinced that another world war would soon erupt. At that moment, being the quite extraordinary visionary that he was, instead of burying hopes of global comity under despair, he resurrected the idea of a global body. He instructed his State Department to start drafting a UN charter but to do so in secret, for he feared, even then, rousing the wrath of American isolationists. Then during the entire five years of World War II, he and the State Department, with the help of members of Congress, worked out the primary principles for this organization.

But Roosevelt first had to overcome the objections of his closest wartime allies, the British and the Soviet Union. Winston Churchill and Joseph Stalin both told him that they preferred, instead of a centralized UN, a series of regional councils—one in Europe, one in the Americas, one in Asia, one in Africa, and so on. However, Roosevelt stuck to his concept of a single all-encompassing organization, and it was his idea that ultimately prevailed.

All of the leaders, though, supported the idea of collective security— the idea of states coming together around common ideals to defend themselves against aggressors. Still, this was not a simple goal to accomplish, as the difficulties with the League of Nations had attested. Eventually, though, Roosevelt drew in both Stalin and Churchill to agree to a mix of idealism and realism in devising the new operational framework of the world body. On the idealistic side, there was now going to be a General Assembly, which would be the forum in which all states, no matter what their size or wealth, would have the right to speak, as well as the right to cast an equal vote with other nations and to control the UN's budget, and gain the UN's legal protection against meddling in their domestic affairs. The assembly's resolutions, nonetheless, would not be binding on member states, though they would carry immense moral force.

On the realist side, the UN Charter attempted to reflect the political realities of the era. It granted five states—the United States, the Soviet Union, China, Great Britain, and France—permanent status on the UN Security Council and, most important, the veto. And then all the signatories to the charter—all the member states—were now obligated to follow any Security Council decision, which represented a truly dramatic change from the old League of Nations, the edicts of which were adhered to only on a voluntary basis.

The argument behind this provision was that only these five countries could supply the military troops, equipment, and financing to undergird UN enforcement actions. It was also a means to end the old ways that the League of Nations had conducted its business, when every nation had the veto and one rogue state could stop any action it disliked. Finally, Roosevelt had one other motive in mind—he wanted to ensure that the U.S. Senate would pass the charter, and the only way he could do that was to guarantee that the United States have a veto in the final accord.

Needless to say, the veto was highly controversial at San Francisco, and of course remains highly controversial today. Many smaller nations objected at the time to limiting the veto to only five states or, in fact, to the existence of any veto. However, in the end, both the United States and the Soviet Union made crystal clear that they would walk out of the conference and leave the UN if they did not get the veto. Given their fierce obstinacy, the smaller states dropped their objections and eventually accepted the deal, believing that it was better to have an organization with the Big Five inside, even possessing the veto power, than to have them outside with no involvement in the UN at all. At the very least, the Big Powers, by being within the UN, could at times be subject to the moral dictates of the organization.

In addition, Roosevelt and his cohorts sought to enhance the authority of the new leader of the UN, the secretary-general. He would be more than just an invisible clerk, which had been true in the days of the League of Nations. The new charter now made him the chief administrative officer and accorded him special authority, under Article 99, "to bring to the attention of the Security Council any matter which, in his opinion, may threaten the maintenance of peace and security." This meant, in effect, that the secretary-general could help initiate debate and, when necessary, propose courses of action—neither of which powers the League had ever granted its own administrative officer. Still, when the UN first began, curiously enough, the majority of observers thought the most powerful position at the UN would always be the presidency of the General Assembly. Indeed, the UN's first secretary-general, Trygve Lie, unsuccessfully sought that post initially, but having lost it, settled reluctantly for what he saw as the lesser job of secretary-general.

Finally, Roosevelt made three other decisions of immense consequence for the success of the conference. First, he won Stalin's agreement to hold the meeting while World War II was still going on. Roosevelt calculated that, as long as the struggle was continuing, all of the representatives coming to San Francisco would take their work more seriously, but the moment the war ended, most would return to their lands to start the reconstruction of their societies, governments, and economies and let the UN slide away.

Second, Roosevelt made certain that the gathering focused only on signing a charter, not on a peace treaty. One of the League of Nation's principal weaknesses had been that, at the Versailles peace conference, its presence got entangled in geopolitical arguments over territorial boundaries and ethnic disputes, which in the end proved fatal.

Third, for the consumption of his own public, Roosevelt insisted that the American delegation going to San Francisco be bipartisan, an equal number of Republicans and Democrats. Wilson had, for his part, filled his delegation mainly with Democrats so that, when the League of Nations treaty came back to the U.S. Senate, the Republican Party had no investment in its passage. Roosevelt thus enlisted such well-known Republicans as John Foster Dulles, Nelson Rockefeller, Harold Stassen, and Senator Arthur Vandenberg. Their participation gave the Republicans a huge reason to enact the final San Francisco treaty.

Roosevelt also poured an immense amount of U.S. resources into hosting the gathering in San Francisco. He flew delegations from war-torn nations that had no available transportation in U.S. military planes to California. He brought in Broadway theatrical craftsmen to design the glittering settings for the conference. He had draftsmen produce the logo and emblem for the UN flag and for its offices: The United States provided hotel rooms, escort personnel, food supplies, daily newspapers, even a library for the delegates. And in the days just before the UN meeting began, Roosevelt himself began to confide in his closest associates that he hoped to be the first UN secretary-general, so deeply was his heart set on its creation. It was, in his mind, to be his greatest legacy and America's most important gift to the world. But it was his final act.

For then, thirteen days before the conference opened, Franklin Roosevelt died, and America and the world faced a crossroads. There was now a new leader in the White House, an enigmatic and still unknown politician named Harry Truman. He was a former senator who had never attended college, had been abroad once in his life when he fought in the first world war and otherwise had had no serious involvement in international affairs. But this unusual man had carried, neatly folded up in his pocket since his youth, a poem by Alfred Lord Tennyson titled "Locksley Hall," which extolled the notion of achieving global peace through "the parliament of man, the Federation of the World." Truman, indeed, turned out to be one of the great internationalist presidents the United States has ever known.

His first decision as president was to instruct that the conference go forward. Later he wrote proudly in his memoirs of his joy in giving that official order. In retrospect, it would have seemed, of course, an entirely logical thing to do. But Truman at that time really had a choice. He could well have said, at that moment, that the United States was not going to participate in a global body. Instead, as the most powerful country on the planet in 1945, Truman could have decided to go down the route of supporting so-called coalitions of the willing, a concept of which Washington is sometimes enamored. But he believed that the world needed a permanent institution to guarantee the peace. Coalitions, in his view, might vanish or break up at any time, but the UN would stay on as a solid pillar of peace in stormy weather and in bright sunshine, in good days and in bad days.

Once the conference began, Truman kept in touch with his delegation on a daily basis. There was a need to do so, for the meeting almost collapsed at least a half dozen times in internal disputes, any of which could have proven to be the death knell for the organization.

There were, first, confrontations about the admissions of certain states. Only states that had declared war against the Axis powers were originally to be admitted. But the Western nations opposed Poland's admission on the grounds it was a crypto-communist state; the Soviets had raised havoc over Argentina's admission on the grounds it was a crypto-Nazi country. However, after painful and very public struggles, both nations were finally allowed membership in the UN. There was also another very public tussle over whom should be the president of the conference. Normally the host nation has the presidency, in this case, the United States. But the Soviet Union wanted all five veto states to share the leadership. Eventually all five agreed to rotate the presidency.

There were, of course, also, as I mentioned earlier, the angry fights over the veto between the big states and the smaller ones. But even among the veto nations themselves, there was a dispute about how broad the veto should be. The Soviets desired an absolute veto that would have blocked any discussion of even a crisis in the Security

Council, and the West insisted on a more limited version of the veto that would not apply to discussion. Eventually it took Truman's sending Harry Hopkins to Moscow for a showdown meeting with Stalin to come to agreement whereby the Soviets backed down on their position and the more limited veto came into being.

There were questions about whether regional organizations should be part of the UN. The Latin countries demanded recognition for their regional body, which later became the Organization of American States. They even threatened to leave the meeting if they could not get their way. Their threat was so startling and alarming that the UN agreed immediately to adopt Article 51, which today permits regional bodies to be part of the organization. Finally there was a grave face-off over the powers of the General Assembly in international crises. A compromise was reached granting to the Assembly more leeway to be involved in issuing pronouncements on global conflicts.

On the final day of the conference, President Harry Truman delivered an impassioned speech, one for the ages: "The successful use of this instrument will require the united will and firm determination of the free peoples who have created it. The job will tax the moral strength and fiber of us all. We all have to recognize, no matter how great our strength, that we must deny ourselves the license to do always as we please. No one nation, no regional group, can or should expect any special privilege which harms any other nation. If any nation would keep security for itself, it must be ready and willing to share security with all. That is the price which each nation will have to pay for world peace. Unless we are willing to pay that price, no organization for world peace can accomplish its purpose. And what a reasonable price that is."

Why did San Francisco succeed in the end? I believe that, in a sense, there was no other choice. The mindset of the delegates in California in the spring of 1945 was almost self-evident. The planet had just endured the two worst catastrophes ever to afflict the earth: World War I, in which some thirty million died, and World War II, in which approximately sixty million lost their lives.

The delegates in San Francisco were simply not willing to accept the possibility of a third violent cataclysm. This was even before they knew about the existence of the atomic bomb. So the delegates were single-minded about constructing a viable global institution that could head off further bloodshed and, fundamentally, save the human species from extinction. So they signed the charter. In the United States, just a month later, the U.S. Senate passed the treaty by the extraordinary margin of 89 to 2.

Could this organization be recreated today? I wonder. I simply do not believe that the peoples of this globe, now consisting of 193 states, would ever come to a common agreement again on principles for a body of this sort. This planet really took advantage of one astonishing moment in history, a wondrous coming together of unique circumstances to devise this assembly. A millisecond earlier or a millisecond later, and the UN would never have happened. And so today it remains the only body of this sort, flaws and all, that we have in our world. To paraphrase Winston Churchill's famous comment about democracy, "it is the worst of all systems except for all the others." It is now up to us to preserve this institution for as long as humankind will endure.

About the Contributors

Editor:

Abiodun Williams is president of the Hague Institute for Global Justice. Previously, he was senior vice president of the Center for Conflict Management at the U.S. Institute of Peace (USIP) and led USIP's work in major conflict zones such as Afghanistan, Iraq, Pakistan, and Libya. Before joining USIP, he served as associate dean of the Africa Center for Strategic Studies at the National Defense University. From 2001 to 2007, he served as director of strategic planning in the Office of the United Nations Secretary-General. He held political and humanitarian affairs positions in U.N. peacekeeping missions in Bosnia and Herzegovina, Haiti, and Macedonia from 1994 to 2000. Williams began his career as an academic and taught international relations at the Edmund A. Walsh School of Foreign Service, Georgetown University, University of Rochester, and Tufts University. Williams is chair of the Academic Council on the UN System, and a board member of the American Bar Association Africa Council of the Rule of Law Initiative. He holds an

MA (Hons) from Edinburgh University, and MALD and PhD degrees from The Fletcher School of Law and Diplomacy, Tufts University.

Contributor:

Kofi A. Annan was the seventh secretary-general of the United Nations, serving two terms from January 1, 1997, to December 31, 2006. In 2001, Kofi Annan and the United Nations were jointly awarded the Nobel Prize for Peace. In addition to his work with the Kofi Annan Foundation, Annan serves as the chairman of the Africa Progress Panel, the Alliance for a Green Revolution in Africa, and as an active member of the Elders. He is also a board, patron, or honorary member of a number of organizations. Mr. Annan currently serves as the chancellor of the University of Ghana, a global fellow at Columbia University in the United States, and Li Ka Shing Professor at the Lee Kuan Yew School of Public Policy at the National University of Singapore. Mr. Annan joined the UN system in 1962 as an administrative and budget officer with the World Health Organization in Geneva. He later served with the Economic Commission for Africa in Addis Ababa, the UN Emergency Force in Ismailia, and the United Nations High Commissioner for Refugees in Geneva. Immediately before becoming secretary-general, he was under-secretary-general for peacekeeping.

Lecturers:

Chinua Achebe played a seminal role in the founding and development of African literature. As a Nigerian writer, he is most well known for the groundbreaking 1958 novel *Things Fall Apart*, a novel still considered to be required reading the world over. Today, this critique is recognized as one of the most generative interventions on Conrad, and one that opened the social study of literary texts, particularly the impact of power relations on twentieth century literary imagination. Achebe is distinguished in his substantial and weighty investment in the building of literary arts institutions. His work as the founding editor of the Heinemann African Writers Series led to his editing more than one hundred titles in it. Achebe also edited the University of Nsukka journal *Nsukkascope,* founded *Okike: A Nigerian Journal of New Writing*, and assisted in the founding of Nwamife Books publishing house, an organization responsible for publishing other groundbreaking work by award-winning writers.

Kwame Anthony Appiah is a member of the Princeton University faculty, where he has appointments in the Philosophy Department and the University Center for Human Values. He joined the Princeton faculty in 2002 as Laurance S. Rockefeller University Professor of Philosophy. Appiah has taught at Yale, Cornell, Duke, and Harvard universities and lectured at many other institutions in the United States, Germany, Ghana, and South Africa, as well as at the École des Hautes Études en Sciences Sociales in Paris. Appiah is widely published in African and African-American literary and cultural studies. He is also the general editor of the Amnesty International Global Ethics Series, published by W. W. Norton. In 2007, Appiah was the president of the eastern division of the American Philosophical Association and served as chair of the APA's executive board from 2008 to 2011. For six years, ending in 2012, he was chair of the board of the American Council of Learned Societies. In March 2009, he succeeded Francine Prose as president of the PEN American Center, a position he held for three years. Appiah was educated at Clare College, Cambridge University, where he received BA and PhD degrees in the philosophy department.

Jagdish Bhagwati is university professor, economics and law, at Columbia University and senior fellow in international economics at the Council on Foreign Relations. He has uniquely combined seminal scientific contributions to the postwar theory of commercial policy, strengthening greatly the case for free trade, with several bestselling books and op-ed essays in leading newspapers and magazines on current trade policy issues. He has been economic policy adviser to the director general, GATT (1991–93) and special adviser to the UN on globalization. He has received several honorary degrees and awards, among them the Freedom Prize (Switzerland), the Bernhard Harms Prize (Germany), and the Thomas Schelling Award (Kennedy School, Harvard). His honors also include high civilian awards from the governments of India (Padma Vibhushan) and Japan (Order of the Rising Sun: Gold and Silver). Among his many successful books is *In Defense of Globalization*.

Leon Botstein has been president of Bard College since 1975. The author of *Jefferson's Children: Education and the Promise of American Culture*, he has been a pioneer in linking American higher education with public secondary schools. Botstein has been the music director of the

American Symphony Orchestra since 1992 and was appointed the music director of the Jerusalem Symphony Orchestra, the orchestra of the Israel Broadcast Authority, in 2003. He is the founder and an artistic director of the Bard Music Festival, now in its twenty-first year. A member of the American Philosophical Society, Botstein has received the Carnegie Corporation Academic Leadership Award, the Award for Distinguished Service to the Arts from the American Academy of Arts and Letters, Harvard University's Centennial Award, and the Austrian Cross of Honour for Science and Art. Botstein received a BA with special honors in history from the University of Chicago and an MA and PhD in European history from Harvard.

Ali Mazrui is Albert Schweitzer Professor in the Humanities and director of the Institute of Global Cultural Studies at Binghamton University, State University of New York. He is also Albert Luthuli Professor-at-Large at the University of Jos in Nigeria. He is Andrew D. White Professor-at-Large Emeritus and senior scholar in Africana Studies at Cornell University. Mazrui has also been appointed chancellor of the Jomo Kenyatta University of Agriculture and Technology in Kenya. Mazrui obtained his BA with distinction from Manchester University in England, his MA from Columbia University in New York, and his doctorate from Oxford University in England. For ten years he was at Makerere University, Kampala, Uganda, where he served as head of the department of political science, dean of the faculty of social sciences as well as dean of the faculty of law. He once served as vice president of the International Political Science Association and has lectured in five continents.

Toni Morrison is the Robert F. Goheen Professor in the Humanities, Emerita, special consultant to the director of the Princeton Atelier, and lecturer with the rank of professor in the Lewis Center for the Arts at Princeton University. Her nine major novels, *The Bluest Eye*, *Sula*, *Song of Solomon*, *Tar Baby*, *Beloved*, *Jazz*, *Paradise*, *Love*, and *A Mercy*, have received extensive critical acclaim. She received the National Book Critics Award in 1978 for *Song of Solomon* and the 1988 Pulitzer Prize for *Beloved*. In 2006, *Beloved* was chosen by the *New York Times Book Review* as the best work of American fiction published in the last quarter century. In 1993, Morrison received the Nobel Prize in Literature.

She graduated from Howard University in 1953 with a BA in English and received a master's degree in 1955 from Cornell University.

Paul Muldoon was educated in Armagh and at the Queen's University of Belfast. From 1973 to 1986 he worked in Belfast as a radio and television producer for the British Broadcasting Corporation. Since 1987, he has lived in the United States, where he is now Howard G.B. Clark '21 Professor at Princeton University and founding chair of the Lewis Center for the Arts. Between 1999 and 2004, he was professor of poetry at the University of Oxford. In 2007 he was appointed poetry editor of *The New Yorker*. Muldoon's main collections of poetry are *New Weather* (1973), *Mules* (1977), *Why Brownlee Left* (1980), *Quoof* (1983), *Meeting The British* (1987), *Madoc: A Mystery* (1990), *The Annals of Chile* (1994), *Hay* (1998), *Poems 1968–1998* (2001), *Moy Sand and Gravel* (2002), *Horse Latitudes* (2006), and *Maggot* (2010).

Seyyed Hossein Nasr, currently university professor of Islamic studies at the George Washington University, Washington, D.C., is a scholar of Islamic, religious, and comparative studies. Possessor of an impressive academic and intellectual record, his career as a teacher and scholar spans more than four decades. Nasr graduated from Massachusetts Institute of Technology with an undergraduate degree in physics and mathematics. He studied geology and geophysics at Harvard University where he completed a PhD in the history of science and philosophy. He has published more than twenty books and hundreds of articles in numerous languages and translations. He has trained different generations of students over the years since 1958 when he was a professor at Tehran University and then, in America since the Iranian revolution in 1979, specifically at Temple University in Philadelphia from 1979 to 1984 and at the George Washington University since 1984.

Daphne Preuss is the CEO and cofounder of Chromatin Inc., a biotechnology company that develops and markets technology for the agricultural, energy, chemical, and nutritional sectors. Before joining Chromatin, Preuss was at the University of Chicago, where she is the Albert D. Lasker Professor of Molecular Genetics and Cell Biology and was previously a Howard Hughes Medical Investigator. Preuss earned a PhD from MIT and performed postdoctoral work at Stanford. Over the course of her academic and business careers, Preuss has developed expertise in plant genetics, genomics, and agricultural biotechnology. In 2000, she chaired the oversight committee for the multinational project that sequenced the first plant genome, and from 2003 to 2006 she chaired the NIH Board of the National Center for Biotechnology Information (NCBI), the institute that maintains data resulting from global efforts in DNA sequencing.

Jeffrey Sachs has been the director of the Earth Institute of Columbia University since 2002. Before his arrival at Columbia University in July 2002, Sachs spent more than twenty years as a professor at Harvard University, most recently as director of the Center for International Development and the Galen L. Stone Professor of International Trade. He is special adviser to United Nations Secretary-General Ban Ki-moon on the Millennium Development Goals (MDGs), having held the same position under former UN Secretary-General Kofi Annan. He is co-founder and chief strategist of Millennium Promise Alliance, and is director of the Millennium Villages Project. He has advised dozens of heads of state, governments, and international organizations on economic strategy. Since the adoption of the MDGs in 2000, Sachs has been the leading academic scholar and practitioner on them.

Stephen Schlesinger is a fellow at the Century Foundation. He is the former director of the World Policy Institute at the New School from 1997 to 2006 and former publisher of the quarterly magazine *The World Policy Journal*. Mr. Schlesinger received his BA from Harvard University and his JD from Harvard Law School. In the early 1970s, he edited and published *The New Democrat Magazine*. Thereafter he spent four years as a staff writer at *Time Magazine*. In the mid-1990s, he worked at the United Nations at Habitat, the agency dealing with global cities. He is the author of three books, including *Act of Creation: The Founding of the United Nations* (2003). He is a specialist on the United Nations and on the foreign policies of the Clinton, Bush, and Obama administrations.

William F. Schulz is acting president and CEO of the Unitarian Universalist Service Committee, a senior fellow at the Center for American Progress specializing in human rights, and served as a consultant to a variety of foundations, including the MacArthur Foundation, UN Foundation, Kellogg Foundation, and Humanity United. He is an adjunct professor of public administration at New York University's Wagner School of Public Service and an affiliated professor at Meadville Lombard Theological School at the University of Chicago. From 1994 to 2006, Schulz served as executive director of Amnesty International USA. During twelve years at Amnesty, Schulz led missions to Liberia, Tunisia, Northern Ireland, and Sudan. He holds a master's degree in philosophy from the University of Chicago and a doctor of ministry degree from Meadville/Lombard Theological School at the University of Chicago.

Amartya Sen is both Thomas W. Lamont University Professor and professor of economics and philosophy at Harvard University and was until 2004 the master of Trinity College, Cambridge. He is also senior fellow at the Harvard Society of Fellows. Earlier on, he was professor of economics at Jadavpur University Calcutta, the Delhi School of Economics, and the London School of Economics, and Drummond Professor of Political Economy at Oxford University. Amartya Sen has served as president of the Econometric Society, the American Economic Association, the Indian Economic Association, and the International Economic Association. He was formerly honorary president of OXFAM. His research has included social choice theory, economic theory, ethics and political philosophy, welfare economics, theory of measurement, decision theory, development economics, public health, and gender studies.

Joseph Stiglitz is professor at Columbia University and chair of Columbia University's Committee on Global Thought. He has taught at Princeton, Stanford, MIT, and was the Drummond Professor and a fellow of All Souls College, Oxford. Stiglitz is also the cofounder and executive director of the Initiative for Policy Dialogue at Columbia. In 2001, he was awarded the Nobel Prize in economics for his analyses of markets with asymmetric information, and he was a lead author of the 1995 Report of the Intergovernmental Panel on Climate Change, which shared the 2007 Nobel Peace Prize. Stiglitz was a member of the Council of Economic Advisers from 1993 to 1995, during the Clinton administration, and served as CEA chairman from 1995 to 1997. He then became chief economist and senior vice president of the World Bank from 1997 to 2000. In 2009, he was appointed by the president of the United Nations General Assembly as chair of the Commission of Experts on Reform of the International Financial and Monetary System. A graduate of Amherst College, Stiglitz received his PhD from MIT in 1967, became a full professor at Yale in 1970, and in 1979 was awarded the John Bates Clark Award.

Jennifer Thomson is emeritus professor in the department of molecular and cell biology at the University of Cape Town. Her main research interests are the development of maize resistant to viruses and tolerant to drought. She has published two books, *Genes for Africa: Genetically Modified Crops in the Developing World*, and *GM Crops: The Impact and the Potential*. Thomson has a BSc in Zoology from UCT, an MA in Genetics from Cambridge, and a PhD in microbiology from Rhodes University. She was a postdoctoral fellow at Harvard Medical School. She was a lecturer, senior lecturer, and associate professor at the University of the Witwatersrand, and director of the CSIR Laboratory for Molecular and Cell Biology, before becoming professor and head of the department of microbiology at the University of Cape Town.

Desmond Tutu earned a teaching diploma from the Pretoria Bantu Normal College by 1954, and later completed a BA degree from the University of South Africa. He was ordained as a deacon in 1960 and became a priest in 1961. In 1962, he moved to London, where he completed his honors and master's degrees in theology in 1966. In 1970, he was offered a lecturing position at Roma University in Lesotho. In 1970, he was appointed associate director of the Theological Education Fund of the World Council of Churches in Kent, England. In 1975, he returned to South Africa to take up the post of Anglican Dean of Johannesburg. Between 1976 and 1978 Tutu was the bishop of the Anglican Church in Lesotho and the general secretary of the South African Council of Churches. Tutu spoke out against the injustice of apartheid and in 1984 he was awarded the Nobel Peace Prize for his efforts. In 1985, he was appointed the bishop of Johannesburg and a year later became the first black cleric to lead the Anglican Church in South Africa when he was named archbishop of Cape Town. Archbishop Tutu continues to campaign vigorously for human rights throughout the world.

Eric Wieschaus is the Squibb Professor in molecular biology at Princeton University. Wieschaus, Edward B. Lewis, and Christiane Nüsslein-Volhard shared the 1995 Nobel Prize in Physiology or Medicine for their work in genetic control of embryonic development. In 1978, Wieschaus was offered a job at the newly established European Molecular Biology Laboratory (EMBL) in Heidelberg. Together with Nüsslein-Volhard, he carried out large-scale mutagenesis experiments to find developmental Drosophila mutants. The result of their work was a new understanding of the mechanism involved in early Drosophila development. In 1981, Wieschaus accepted a position at Princeton University and his research continues to focus on development, specifically on changes in cell shape during the various developmental stages. Wieschaus received his BA in biology from Notre Dame and his PhD from Yale University in 1974.

About the Institute

The United States Institute of Peace is an independent, nonpartisan institution established and funded by Congress. Its goals are to help prevent and resolve violent conflicts, promote postconflict peacebuilding, and increase conflict management tools, capacity, and intellectual capital worldwide. The Institute does this by empowering others with knowledge, skills, and resources, as well as by its direct involvement in conflict zones around the globe.